Storm of Terror

STORM OF TERROR

A Hebron Mother's Diary

June Leavitt

IVAN R. DEE

CHICAGO 2002

Library of Congress Cataloging-in-Publication Data:
Leavitt, June O.
    Storm of terror : a Hebron mother's diary / June Leavitt.
        p. cm.
    ISBN 1-56663-467-9 (alk. paper)
    1. Leavitt, June O.—Diaries. 2. Jews, American—West Bank—Hebron—Diaries. 3. Arab-Israeli conflict—1993—West Bank—Hebron—Personal narratives, American. 4. Arab-Israeli conflict—1993—West Bank—Hebron—Personal narratives, Israeli. I. Title.

DS113.8.A4 L435 2002
956.95'1044—dc21   2002067391

In memory of all the victims of terrorism

and their families

To my husband, my soul mate. To our old children, Shmulik, Yossi, Estie, Yehoshua, and Miriam, and our new ones, Adi, Shachar, and Oriah, whose energy and love make all things possible in this world.

To Neil Amdur, who through the decades has been a staunch and loyal friend, my deepest thanks. When the sky opened up, he was there. Without him, my diaries would not have been brought to light.

My deep thanks to Marilyn Amdur, my stepsister, who is really much more than that. Through the years she has encouraged me and given me confidence and strength.

J. L.

Kiriat Arba, Israel
May 2002

Storm of Terror

In the *goldener medina,* Isaac from Minsk knew Ida from Pinsk, and she became pregnant and had Claire.

And in the *goldener medina,* Joseph from Oppenheim knew Betty from Taubersbisopsheim and she had Jerome.

And Claire went out from her house in Brooklyn. And Jerome went out from his house on Sherman Avenue. They met and they married, and after eight years of marriage, Claire became pregnant and she had two children.

One child became a prominent real estate lawyer—handsome, brilliant, and rich. For his weekend pleasure he bought a small estate far out on Long Island and for the other days of the week maintained an elegant bachelor apartment in the most fashionable district of Manhattan.

The other became a settler in the West Bank of Israel. For years, to the disgrace and fear of her family, she has lived in the violence surrounding Kiriat Arba, a settlement near Hebron, with her husband and five children.

No one can believe that this brother and sister came from the same mother and father. As children, raised in a wealthy neighborhood on Long Island, they romped in the same large house, ate the same steaks broiled by the housekeeper, and went to the same posh summer camps even though they had a swimming pool right in their own backyard.

In June 1968 her brother Robert paddled on one raft and she lay back on another wearing her shocking-pink bikini, one hand plunged into the water, the other on her abdomen. She was putting the finishing touches on the golden tan she so desperately needed for the senior prom. She was determined to be the most attractive girl there. She had bought a brightly patterned silk lounging dress at Macy's on Thirty-fourth Street, after seeing it advertised in the *New York Times*. Her much older boyfriend, dapper and bronzed, would pick her up in his blue Thunderbird convertible. On his arm, she would be the envy of all.

Floating on the pool's calm, she was unaware of deep forces, within and without, that would change the surface of all things.

"Trunk's packed?" Robert asked.

"Full to the brim." Her college trousseau had cost a fortune. For each dress or suit she had bought matching leather shoes.

"Are you happy about going to college?" her brother asked.

"Of course." She was going to major in journalism, then make a lucrative career of writing.

It was all so clear, a well-defined path with the landmarks all laid out for her by her mother before she died.

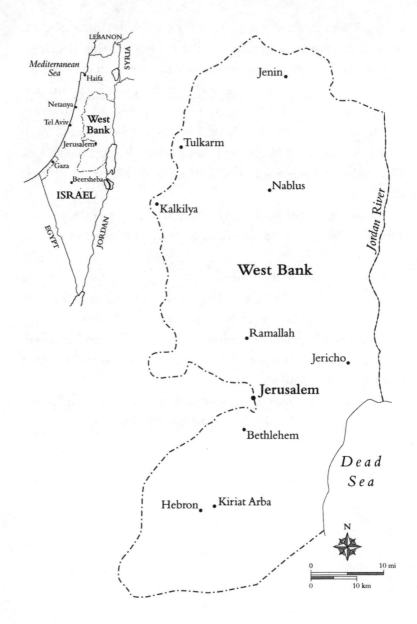

Kiriat Arba, Hebron, September 30, 2000

Phones don't usually ring on Rosh Hashanah. Instead, *shofars* are blown from every synagogue to remind us that the first ten days of Tishrei are days of judgment. The first of these is Rosh Hashanah, the New Year, when God balances the scales of good deeds and bad for each Jew and for the entire Jewish nation. Who will become rich and who will become poor? Who will live and who will die?

But this Rosh Hashanah it was difficult to hear the *shofars* over the sound of gunfire. More clearly, I heard the phone ring. Estie jumped up. She knew it was for her. I watched her go to the phone. At just about the same age I floated idly on the swimming pool in my pink bikini. She was in skintight knickers that hung three inches below her navel. Her navel was pierced with three jewels. We have been told that we have the same facial structure—a bit square in the jaw, high cheekbones, a sharp straight nose. But our coloring is different; she is pale with a freckled nose and light blue eyes.

Yet there are differences far less superficial. She's seen many people die. People she loved. At her age I was a sophomore in college; I was not serving in the Israeli army.

A few months ago, coming home one night from Jerusalem, I saw an ambulance pulled up in front of our house. Walking inside, I encountered a medic coming out of my daughters' room.

Miriam, Estie's younger sister, tried to comfort me. "Don't worry. Estie is all right. She's just resting."

"Resting? But what's she doing home? She's in training!"

Miriam replied, "When Yossi went to visit her at her base he found her not feeling well, so he brought her home. But when her fever went way up and she started vomiting, I called Emergency."

The medic said to me sympathetically, "She was bitten in the navel by a scorpion. It was a yellow one, the most dangerous kind, especially now, in spring. She has to get to the hospital quickly."

"She has to get to the hospital quickly." Dr. Baruch Goldstein muttered those very same words to us years ago when Estie had come down with a rare infectious disease. My head was spinning between past and the present. Now I heard the words, "I ordered an ambulance."

Once again, Estie was rushed to the hospital. This time her body was swollen and her fine-boned face was puffy beyond recognition. We sat by her bed for four days.

And when she got better, she resumed her training to become a combat soldier in Israel's first unit of women combat soldiers since the 1950s.

Soon she was sent to Hebron. Although she was coming home, we weren't happy. We wanted her far away from here, far away from the violence that has shaken this ancient city of mildewed stones. Many of our friends and neighbors have been killed and rest forever here beneath their oblong tombstones. And the people who live here fight to stay above the ground.

Just two months ago, on a Shabbat afternoon, one of Miriam's friends was grabbed and kissed by an Arab on the steps leading into Kiriat Arba. She managed to escape. When the word spread that a girl had been molested by an Arab and that the police hadn't handled it aggressively, the Jewish settlers of Hebron rioted.

Miriam took part in the riots, which Estie had to quell. Settlers threw stones at Arab cars and shop windows. The next day, in retaliation, the Arabs rioted, throwing bottles at Israeli soldiers. They burned tires and advanced on Israeli soldiers' positions. They began hitting and striking them with clubs and fists. Estie suddenly found herself separated from her unit. When she called for help on the military radio, she found she had no communication at all. The patrol that preceded her had failed to recharge the battery.

She considered firing her rifle but thought better of it. So five-foot-two Estie, who looked a little larger in her helmet and green fatigues, started screaming at the Arabs to back off. As she screamed, Miriam and the settlers were advancing on her position yelling that the Israeli soldiers were "castrated puppets of the peace." When they got close enough, some of the settlers even spit at her.

A few days later, exhausted, angry, and frayed, Estie came home for a rest. As soon as she walked in the door, an explosion erupted between her and her younger sister. "Don't you ever come down to Hebron again while I'm there!"

"Of course I'm going to come down! You think I'm going to let the Arabs take it over and not try to do anything about it?"

Miriam, her younger sister, towers over Estie. She is five feet nine inches tall with a head of massive curly hair. Miriam has become ultra-Orthodox and fanatically right-wing. She wears long sleeves and ankle-length skirts and prays with fervor three times a day. Miriam favors the transfer of the Arabs. Estie favors the transfer of the Jews.

Estie goes around with her three jewels showing. Often she has provoked the righteous anger of her older, religious brother, Yossi, and her younger, extremely religious brother, Yehoshua. When Estie once performed with a jazz group on television, I ran downstairs to call the two boys. Since we don't have a television, I was watching at a neighbor's apartment. One look at Estie on the screen, dancing in a sparse leotard and Yossi, followed by Yehoshua, stormed out of the apartment, hurling an oath from the book of Genesis. "What? Will we allow our sister to be made a whore of?"

Yehoshua (Joshua in English) became religious after the bus he was riding in was attacked by terrorists. He was twelve years old. Coming home from a soccer match in Jerusalem, he put his head on his knees to rest. When the bullets pierced the windows of the bus, one flew over his head and into the back of his best friend, Shalom. When Yehoshua picked his head up, he saw that two men were slumped over with bullets in their heads. One murdered neighbor leaned his head against his pregnant wife's shoulder as she yelled at him to get up.

14

That night, for the first time in his life, Yehoshua put a book of psalms under his pillow. Soon he put a yarmulke on his head. Then he approached the religious high school here and asked to be admitted.

So Yossi and Yehoshua tore down all pictures of the family in bathing suits and removed all CD covers they thought immodest. Yossi accused my husband and me of having too-liberal views which cheapened Estie.

So often I have felt like the helmswoman of a storm-ridden ship. This Rosh Hashanah I prayed for true peace.

We sat down at the festive meal. On Rosh Hashanah we eat all kinds of food whose Hebrew name or quality suggests the goodness we are asking from God—apples dipped in honey, so the year will be sweet; pomegranate seeds so we will be as numerous as they. We were eating morsels of fish head and uttering, "When you judge us, please place us as high as the head, and not as low as the tail," when the phone rang. Estie, who was on call for the army, grabbed the receiver. She didn't have to tell us the message.

Quickly she put on her green fatigues and the helmet with a ceramic shield that protects her head against shrapnel. She picked up her A-3 sharpshooter's rifle, and within minutes a military jeep pulled up outside our apartment house in Kiriat Arba, a few yards away from Hebron. The soldiers inside passed her a heavy bulletproof vest that weighs one-quarter as much as she does. She put it on and tried to smile. I wondered again why she had been so hardheaded, why she had insisted on being combat-ready when she could have done office work as a lot of young women in the Israeli Army do. But of course I knew why. Her oldest brother, Shmulik, is in an elite unit. Yossi was in an elite unit too.

The jeep pulled out into the street. As it did, I heard mobs of Arabs screaming just steps away in Hebron and border police with sirens and megaphones declaring a curfew. I went outside and looked over the ancient city where Abraham buried his Sarah and wept over her. I thought, We have raised all our children here?

And I answered, Here are all the friends I have in the world and all the enemies. Here Miriam and Yehoshua were born. Here we brought Estie when she was six months old, Yossi two and a half, and Shmulik four and a half. This is the only world my children know.

Below I see our Arab neighbor's house. Kais had been my sons' friend. With him, my three sons had raised and pastured their donkeys until the peace process put up barbed wire between us and the Arabs. In the valley I see the animal farm Kais helped my sons build—cages for rabbits and coops for chickens. Maybe they'll meet him on the battlefield one day.

Below on the street I see telling pillars of black smoke. The Arabs are burning tires.

For three days now Arabs have been shooting and fighting with Israeli soldiers all over the country. Several soldiers have been killed and scores of Arabs killed or injured. Roads into Kiriat Arba and Hebron are closed as Arabs take up the weapons that the Rabin government gave them as part of the peace process, and use them against us.

October 2

Estie called to say that she's been given guard duty at her base. I was glad she called. She never answers her cellular phone, and it's almost her birthday.

Nineteen years ago on the Shabbat after her birth, my husband held her in his arms. We made a celebration for her at the settlement of Atzmona in the Sinai desert where we were living. Quoting from the Haftorah portion, he rocked her in his arms and said, "Here, this is the blessing."

Six months later we were evacuated because the Sinai Peninsula was given to Egypt as part of the Camp David Agreement signed by Israel and Egypt in 1977. Exiled, we moved to Hebron. Under Menachem Begin's Likud government, Jewish property in Hebron was being reclaimed from the Arabs. We moved into a decrepit building which had been built a hundred years ago as a *yeshiva* by a wealthy Turkish Jew named Romano. The Turks had taken it over and made it into a jail. After them, the British had turned it into a police station.

When the war of independence broke out in 1948, and the Arabs gained control of the West Bank, they took over the Romano Building and turned it into a school.

In 1982 after a lengthy court procedure in which prior Jewish ownership was demonstrated, the Arabs were evicted from the building. A few days later my husband and I and our three children moved into a room there. Soon our fourth child, Yehoshua, was born.

We buried his circumcised foreskin in the dirt before the Cave of the Patriarchs and Matriarchs. This was symbolic, for buried in the cave are almost all our forefathers and foremothers—Abraham and Sarah, Jacob and Leah, Isaac and Rebecca.

Jewish tradition suggests that Hebron is the most sacred place in the world, more sacred even than Jerusalem. This is because Adam and Eve are also buried in the cave that Abraham bought in Hebron from Ephron the Hittite. He bought it because there was something mystical about the place. The cave is really the door to the Garden of Eden. All Jewish souls when they die must crawl back to the Garden, a task made easier if you are buried nearby.

But there was life here too.

In Hebron, Abraham had his first dream in which God revealed his deep and mysterious plans. In this dream Abraham saw that his descendants would be slaves in Egypt for four hundred years but would then be redeemed. Abraham was so shaken by the dream that he bolted up, made an altar, slaughtered a sheep, and offered a sacrifice.

When King David first assumed the throne, he made Hebron his capital. For seven years he reigned over his entire kingdom from Tel Romeida, one of the highest areas in Hebron.

Now Hebron is in what the Arabs call the West Bank or the "Occupied Territories." The Jews call the area Judea. We have come to call it home.

In 1982, when we moved here, we did not foresee that the very same agreement which exiled us from the Sinai, years later would threaten us again. For in this agreement, Israel had committed herself in principle to giving autonomy to the Arabs in Judea, Samaria, and the Gaza Strip.

When we first moved to Hebron, there were only sporadic incidents of violence. But in 1991, after a new agreement specifying the terms of autonomy to be given to the Arabs was signed in Madrid, it was the periods of quiet that became sporadic. The Intifada uprising had begun.

Then came the Oslo Peace Accords when Prime Minister Yitzhak Rabin finally sat down with Jordan's King Hussein and PLO Chairman Yasser Arafat. Until this time the leaders of Israel had vowed never to sit down with Arafat because there was so much Jewish blood on his hands. Now, on the White House lawn, Rabin shook one of those hands.

After Oslo, the Palestine Liberation Organization (PLO) was no longer a terrorist organization; it was a partner in peace. It would be allowed to form an armed and powerful police force responsible for the enforcement of law and order. On maps, lines were drawn dividing Judea, Samaria, and the Gaza Strip into Arab- or Jewish-controlled areas. Fences were erected and concrete walls were built separating Jews from Arabs. Hebron began to look like Berlin after World War II.

As each stage of the Oslo Peace Accords was implemented Israel pulled back farther from her historic lands. Bethlehem, where King David was born, and all the villages around it went to the Arabs. Jericho, which Joshua conquered, passed into Arab control. Gaza, where Samson had lived and fought the Philistines, was handed over to Arafat and his people and became the capital of what is now called the Palestinian Authority. The port of Gaza was opened to free commerce, and Israel would not be allowed to inspect what was coming in. Shechem was handed over to Yasser Arafat's people, and Israel would maintain control only over the Tomb of Joseph.

And most of Hebron was handed over. Only one street with its three neighborhoods and the hilltop of Tel Romeida, where King David once lived and ruled, were left for the Jews.

Kalachnikov rifles taken from the Arabs in previous wars were distributed by Israel to the new autonomous Arab police. There was hope that they would use them to prevent terrorist attacks against Israel. At the same time, in the Port of Gaza, now free of Israeli control, more powerful weapons were smuggled in by the PLO. Several times Estie's base has come under fire from heavy machine guns. She fires back or, if the bullets come too close, dives into the dirt for cover.

October 3

Miriam has her head on my lap, and I am stroking her hair, aware that I'm not always available for my children. I love them very much, but I'm carrying emotional baggage from my past life in America. My children, ever since they can remember, have had a mother whose mind often seemed to be somewhere else. When I used to go for walks with Miriam, she would cry, "Hold my hand tighter! Tighter!"

Our children must adjust not only to terrorism, but to us.

"Why do you have to go to India?" she asked me. "Now, of all times?"

"You can go. I'll help." Shmulik, short for Shmuel or Samuel, was sitting with us. Our oldest son, he had immigrated with us from America. He had absorbed a minute quantity of our past lives and thoughts and understood us better than our Israeli children, our *sabarim*. He too was getting ready for travel; his four-and-a-half year stint in the submarine service soon would be coming to an end. Now he was looking at maps—he would travel alone for a year.

Shmulik said, "I'll be going back and forth between port and home, so I can watch over Miriam some of the time. When I'm not around, she'll stay with Yossi and Adi in Samaria."

"Please don't go!" Miriam sunk into me.

Aside from the new wave of Arab terror, she was having a terror of her own. She hated to be the only child left in the house. Most families here have at least seven children, some as many as seventeen. There is no such thing as being left alone. There are always brothers and sisters, nephews and nieces around.

Miriam was feeling sorry for herself as it was. Estie had been drafted into the army. Yossi had married and moved away. Shmulik was in the navy. Yehoshua, though only seventeen, was totally independent, and we weren't seeing much of him lately.

"You're going to leave me here alone?"

"You won't be alone. Don't you see?" I pleaded with her. "Your father has this dream about bringing a medical education team to the poorest and most unfortunate people in India. The Untouchables. Did you ever hear of them?"

"Aren't there poor and needy people in Israel?" she asked.

Like most religious Zionists, she is xenophobic. The world has been created for the Jewish people and Israel. The outside world holds little interest. Moreover, as a religious Zionist she believes that a Jew is never supposed to leave the land of Israel. After everything God did to bring us out of Egypt? To leave the land is to put oneself in exile all over again.

Weakly I say, "But Aba wants me to come this time. We planned it a long time ago, before the Arabs started shooting at everybody."

"So let Aba go. *You* don't have to go."

I could feel my resolve collapsing. What if war breaks out while we are gone, separating us from our children? If there is a war, three of our children will be fighting in it!

Yossi is just finishing his three-year tour of army duty, but if there is war he will be called up for reserves. And even if there isn't an all-out war, there is a well full of other worries to draw from. He lives on a lonely mountaintop in Samaria above the ancient city of Shechem with his wife, Adi, who is six months pregnant.

The Arabs refer to the city of Shechem as Nablus. There has been as much violence there recently as there has been in Hebron. In both places, spiritual power seeps up through the mildewed stones. It is not a calming spiritual power. It is the spiritual power that breathes life into the imminent holy war.

I try to calm myself and conquer my fears of holy wars. I reason that by conquering my fears and bearing the most difficult things, that I have always made myself somehow better. Better?

All people want to do the right thing. But how are we to

know what that is? There is such darkness; we live in a fog. All over Israel people are pursuing courses in meditation, bioenergy, and kinesiology, and running to healers of the soul in order to learn how to lift that fog. And once the fog begins to lift, glimmers of truth can be seen.

I get up, go into the bedroom and close the door. I take out two things. One is my pendulum. I meditate for a moment and try to clear my mind.

I ask, "Should I go to India at this time?"

The pendulum swings strongly "yes." Through further questioning it also tells me that the second phase of the Arab uprising will last five years. No point in waiting it out. Our trip will be blessed. The children will survive.

The second is my deck of tarot cards.

I lay out the cards. The central issue of my life, the cards say, (my heart skips a beat) is a man and woman journeying in a little boat. There is a sadness about them. They have left one shore and are headed toward another. This card is crossed by the Hanged Man who hangs upside-down. There is light surrounding his head, however.

Like my journey in search of Indians in Vermont, this trip will turn me upside-down. Yet there is deep purpose in it; it was in Vermont, in the deep of the woods, that I met Frank.

Now Frank says I must make this journey to India. All the plans have been put together, and I am a part of them.

October 15

From the phone shack in the isolated village of Kadalur, I heard from Miriam and Yehoshua about two Israeli reserve soldiers who made a wrong turn and drove into Ramallah. There they were stopped by Palestinian police and brought to police head-quarters where an Arab mob attacked them. They were battered with clubs, pipes, and fists, then thrown head first down two stories into the street.

One died. The other, seriously wounded, was tied to the exhaust pipe of a car and dragged through the streets until he was pulp and bone. Our children told us they had seen it on television, seen Arabs raise their hands full of blood, their arms outstretched in victory.

They also told me about the three Israeli soldiers at Har Dov on the Lebanese border who were kidnapped by Hizballah.

Another time, Frank and I telephoned Yossi.

Yossi cried when he told us that the Israeli army had pulled out of Joseph's Tomb in Shechem, a town which lies in the valley below his house—the very place where Joseph wished that his bones be placed after his death.

Yossi told us that the Israeli army had surrendered the tomb to Palestinian police after a battle in which a Druze border po-liceman was mortally injured. According to the terms of surren-der, the Druze, Madchat Yusuf, was to be evacuated by the Palestinian police and treated in a hospital for his wounds. The tomb itself, according to the terms of the "peace" agreement, would be protected as a Jewish holy place.

Minutes later Yossi saw thick smoke rising out of the tomb. Arabs had set fire to the compound, and Madchat Yusuf was inside. Hillel, a friend of Yossi's, must have seen the smoke too. They surmise that Hillel, unarmed, ran out of his house and down the mountain toward the tomb.

That was the last time Hillel Lieberman, a rabbi and father of seven, was seen alive. Shmulik, on leave from sea duty, went up to help Yossi and other friends on the all-night search, but it was the army who found him in a cave, covered in his bullet-ridden prayer shawl.

When they tried to remove Hillel's body, Arabs fired on the Israeli soldiers. Yossi said that we retaliated by bombing the police headquarters in Ramallah where the lynching of the two Israeli soldiers took place.

October 22

Shmulik, Miriam, and Miriam's best friend picked us up at the airport, but on our way home we heard on our communication radio that the roads to Kiriat Arba, Hebron, were closed because of shooting. As the army hadn't yet sealed off the road, we decided to take a chance.

Except for army jeeps, tanks, and armored personnel carriers, the roads were eerily empty. There was none of the usual traffic of settlers who, all through the years of the first Intifada and despite the stone throwing, persisted in driving their cars with Israeli flags furling from the windows.

During that first Intifada my husband Frank had his eye and jaw smashed by a sharp rock hurled through the window of his car. Surviving that had given him tremendous faith. My fight has been to acquire a faith of my own.

While we were in India, Yehoshua and Shmulik filled bags with sand and piled them on our windowsills. Now our ground-floor apartment is banked for cover against the Arab neighborhood on the southeastern hillside that slopes into Hebron.

We had been on very good terms with some of the Arabs living there. Frank used to sit and drink sweet tea with Shakar. Shakar's children had played with ours in the gully that runs between our houses, until the Clinton-Arafat-Rabin peace process put up that dividing fence topped with coils of sharp wire.

So much has changed here.

Few people go out of their houses. Buses rarely run since the road to Jerusalem has become the scene of many gun battles. This road was built by the Rabin government to bypass Arab towns so that Jews wouldn't have to go through them once they were handed over to Arafat. The towns were supposed to be *judenrein*.

Blinded into optimism by its peace initiative, the Rabin government did not see that the bypass road, running as it did beneath the hillside town of Bait Jala, would be a very vulnerable target if the Palestinian police ever turned their guns against us—the Kalachnikovs that had been given to them by Israel as part of the peace.

Bait Jala, a once peaceful and wealthy Christian-Arab town, has been taken over by Tanzim gunmen—Palestinian police who work by day in law enforcement and at night by gunpoint, driving lawful inhabitants out of their villas. From the window of these villas, which command a view of the bypass road beneath, the Palestinian police fire upon Jewish traffic and fire at the Jerusalem neighborhood of Gilo. There, a border policeman was critically wounded as he drove through the streets.

October 23

Yossi's full name is Yoseph Yehuda Leib, after my grandfather and Frank's grandfather. Our children always tell us that we piled all possible names on him, leaving none to have more children with.

Full of names, he was also so full of mischief that for every name we gave him, he piled a thousand worries on us. He was always moving and roving, on horses, dune buggies, and motorcycles, in a whirl of activity that his peers love and admire. He walks into a room and things happen. The air is charged; for us, too charged. By the time he was thirteen I dreaded the sound of the phone ringing. It would be his school in Jerusalem asking where he was.

"But I put him on the bus this morning!"

"Yes, but he never got here."

We had to send him away to a boarding school. This was very hard for Shmulik because Yossi had been his best friend.

The school was by the sea, and Yossi was drawn to it because he wanted to be a sea commando. But instead of studying
he bought himself a surfboard. During the day he sneaked out of
the school through a hole in the fence. At night he stuffed his
bed. Day and night, fall and winter, he took to the sea. I took to
unplugging the telephone.

But eventually Yossi fared well. At seventeen he put his
physical prowess and chaotic energy into a directed purpose.
Along with his teacher and some classmates, he manned a sail-
boat and sailed to Greece.

Not long after that his childhood dream became a reality. At
age eighteen-and-a-half he was drafted into the sea commandos.
But then something happened, cutting short his long-cherished
dream.

The human being he most admired, Dov Dribben, was
killed.

Dov, lean and mean to whomever made problems for his
people, was the son of Eddie Dribben, the legendary cowboy of
Kiriat Arba. Dov had taught Shmulik and Yossi to ride horses
when they were little.

Dov's parents were among the first settlers to trickle back to
this area after the Six-Day War in 1967 when the Israeli army
beat the Jordanians back from Judea and Samaria. They were living in a cave outside of Hebron in 1970 when his mother went
into labor. Dov came into the world in an army jeep on the dirt
road to Jerusalem and was named after Dov Ettinger, an Israeli
army officer killed on the same road a few months before. Dov
was the first male born to the new settlers of Hebron.

From his boyhood he would climb on his horse and gallop

through Hebron, exploring far-off neighborhoods where Arabs seldom saw Jewish people because the Jewish people were too afraid to go there. Armed with knives and powerful fists, Dov was a fierce and proud Hebrew stepping into life from the parched pages of the Old Testament.

Every time Shmulik and Yossi came home from their military service, the first person they went to see was Dov. Against our will, our son Yehoshua even dropped out of school so that he could work, buy a horse, and ride high, just like Dov.

The name Dov means "bear." And nothing, we thought, could harm a bear. But on April 19, 1998, on the extra day added to the Passover holiday, Dov was building a house on a lonely hilltop for his best friend Phatty, who was about to marry. He saw Arab "shepherds" trespassing onto the land and ran down into the valley unarmed.

Three Arab shepherds were the bait. Eight other Arabs lay in wait. They jumped him, bringing him down onto the rocks and scrub. He fought them bare-handed until Phatty, seeing the skirmish, tore down the hill with his gun. Then another friend ran down. In the fighting, one of the Arabs grabbed the gun and fired.

Both friends were injured. Dov sank into a pool of dust and blood with three bullets in his heart.

When Dov was laid to rest and the last dirt thrown on his open grave, two Jewish riders made a whooping wail, then galloped away through the hills Dov loved, the place where he breathed his dying breath.

Dov had been so proud that Yossi made it into the sea commandos, the toughest, most elite unit in the Israeli military. But

29

Yossi was shattered by Dov's death. He no longer had the concentration he needed for such rigorous training. Confused by the political situation where in the name of peace his friends were cut down, he lost his love of Israel and her defense forces. No longer motivated, he let his dream slip through his fingers.

He never found himself in the army again, but he did find himself in a cave near where Dov was killed.

It is customary here that in the place a settler has been cut down, a new settlement is planted. So, after Dov's murder, Yehoshua and his friends pulled stones from the very same ground to make the foundations for their homes. As they worked, a small Israeli flag, signifying the place where Dov had fallen, snapped in the perpetual wind above the pile of rocks.

A month later a truck brought in their first load of lumber and they put up the frames. After that we rarely saw Yehoshua. He had found a focus in his young life—he would take up where Dov had left off. Yehoshua and his friends built on.

Arafat and Clinton cried out that this violated the Oslo Accords. Jewish settlement activity was to be frozen in the West Bank. But with the support of one Zionist faction in the leftist Israeli government, Yehoshua and his friends lovingly put up the walls, board upon board, leaving large spaces for windows which looked out over the Judean desert plateau. On sunny days they could even see the Dead Sea. Outside, their horses whinnied and stamped their feet.

Far away, in the chambers of power, Prime Minister Barak promised Arafat and Clinton that he meant to keep to the terms of the peace. All new settlements would indeed be dismantled, including the outpost at Maon where Yehoshua and his friends were now raising the roofs, putting on doors, and installing plumbing in their nearly completed homes.

The government gave them an ultimatum: "Move of your own free will into an already existing settlement or we will blow your houses down."

"And give back the land Dov died for?"

Hundreds of settlers came from all over the country to show support and to resist any possible evacuation. Yehoshua's house was taken over by settler girls and women, so he and his friends moved into the corral. Soon even that became crowded.

On November 10, 1999, two thousand soldiers converged on the hilltop outpost of Maon and led hundreds of people away. Yehoshua grabbed the keys to a tractor and tried to block the hordes of soldiers, police, and bulldozers. Thirty people who locked themselves in the house that Dov had been building for Phatty and his bride were arrested.

Yossi, who was there, called me on a cellular phone to tell me that all resistance had been smashed. Military tractors had pushed over Yehoshua's and Phatty's houses. The corral was in a rubble. The horses and dogs had been evacuated too.

That afternoon Yossi, broken once again, came home. We did not hear from Yehoshua.

The next day Miriam went to look for him. She found him sitting on the hilltop with other stragglers, crying. Then he threw stones at the rubble. Yossi returned to him with food I had cooked and they spent the night there in a cave.

Caves are plentiful in the limestone hills around Hebron, and near the devastation is a series of them on a grassy terrace graced by olive trees. By the Sabbath, many settlers, including

Yossi, Yehoshua, and Miriam, had regrouped in these caves with food, drink, and sleeping bags. They called their new enclave "Cave City." Yossi didn't tell me that there, a young settler woman, tall, with dark slanting eyes and dark silken hair, had caught his eye.

Then I heard that "Cave City" had also been evacuated. I heard that although the Israeli government had promised that the Maon outpost would become a closed military area, Arabs were grazing their flocks there and had even begun to till the soil. I knew that skirmishes had broken out between the frustrated and angry settlers and Arabs. I knew that many people on both sides had been injured. I knew Jews who had been arrested.

My children had come to believe that life was meaningless, that Dov had died for nothing.

Two months later the phone rang in the middle of the night. Frank was in India again and the sound of the phone sent shock waves down to my marrow. Yossi got up and took the call. I was just getting back to sleep when the phone rang again and Yossi began speaking in a soft voice.

I jumped out of bed and asked him who it was. He didn't want to tell me.

"You either tell me, or I'll tell him to stop calling at this hour! It is one-thirty in the morning!"

He smiled an embarrassed smile. "I just got an answer," he said.

"At this hour? An answer to what?"

"If she wanted to marry me."

"Who? *What?*"

"I'm getting married, Ema."

"To whom?"

"Adi. I met her in a cave."

A young couple just seven months married shouldn't have to narrate such things. Yossi and Adi didn't want to tell us while we were away in India. So they called us now.

On a mount facing theirs, Mt. Eval, where God stood many lifetimes ago and said that whoever is blessed will go there, forty Israelis went on an outing. Just as they stepped out of their bus and began to ascend, Arab gunmen from a nearby village shot at them. Men, women, and children ran for cover, but many were seriously injured.

Binyamin Herling, Yossi and Adi's rabbi, fired back with an Uzi until a bullet struck him. My son watched Israeli helicopters try to evacuate him and the others, but Arabs shot at the helicopters, and gun battles continued for hours. Binyamin Herling bled to death.

I pray things will quiet down. Estie is now stationed at Bait Hadassah in the Jewish quarter of Hebron; Yossi and his pregnant wife live on the hill above Joseph's burned-out tomb; so many of those we know are now widowed and orphaned; roads are closed and Arab gunmen lie in wait. I teach English three days a week in Jerusalem. How will I get there? And how will I return? How will Frank get to the university in Beer Sheba where he teaches, and how will he return? Will we return covered with the Israeli flag?

Yet I pray with only half a heart. The other half tells me there is a cancer in this land—a cancer that began over five thousand years ago when Abraham's barren wife Sarah told him to lie with her handmaid Hagar so that he could have children. Hagar gave birth to Ishmael, and shortly after, Sarah herself became pregnant and gave birth to Yitzhak (Isaac).

But Ishmael always taunted Yitzhak, Jewish tradition tells us. And because Sarah was jealous of Hagar, she made Abraham drive out the handmaid and her son. As Hagar sat crying in the wilderness, God came to her and made an ambiguous promise. As he had once promised Abraham, he now promised to make of Ishmael a great nation too.

Arab Moslems claim they are the spiritual heirs of Abraham through his son Ishmael. Many Jews say this is not true, that Arabs are not really the descendants of Ishmael at all.

Now God's ambiguous promise has erupted into a violent disease. The peace process was a way to suppress the disease, but it has showed up more virulent than ever. What is needed is a cleansing; but a cleansing might require a painful, full-scale war with all Arab nations to decide the rightful inheritor of Abraham.

All realities here have roots which extend deep into the past. And I'm trying to understand and disentangle them all. I, the daughter of an American Jewish mother who hated Judaism with her life, who before her death made me promise never to wear a Jewish star.

November 6

When American Jews were glued to their radios and televisions with the outbreak of the Six-Day War in Israel, I was joyfully taking off the flower corsages that had been pinned on me for my seventeenth birthday. The only thought I had was that the corsages had been plentiful. I was a popular girl brought up in such an assimilated fashion that I didn't even notice any differences between me and the Gentiles with whom I went to school.

The word "Israel" was not in our lexicon. We didn't know where such a country was, and we didn't care. Which is just what my mother wanted.

My mother's parents were Russian immigrants. They made *aliya* to Brooklyn and not to Israel. They were so proud of my mother. She was beautiful and bright. She married my father who, at the age of twenty-five, was already making a great deal of money selling costume jewelry. She didn't have to live in the flat above the family's hardware store in Brooklyn. She and my father installed themselves in a stately apartment in Gramercy Park.

And four years later they did what had been unthinkable in Minsk or Pinsk or Oppenheim. They went to live near the Gentile aristocracy in a big and stately house.

When I wanted to put Chanukah lights in our window as some of my friends in less expensive neighborhoods did, my mother wouldn't allow it. I was not even given a Hebrew name when I was born, a secret name that most Jewish parents give.

My mother's secret name was Esther and we gave this name to our daughter, Estie. My mother would turn over in her grave if she knew her secrets were revealed.

When she was dying at the age of forty, her venetian blinds shut against the swimming pool outside where her friends played canasta, she called me into her room. Delirious, she asked me if I had grown pubic hair. Then she mumbled something about Russia and pogroms, which I, a ten-year-old child, could not understand. She had never seen Russia and certainly never a pogrom.

Now I understand. People inherit memories, and those memories can rule their lives.

Was God trying to show my mother that she could not defy destiny? While she might have repressed her own fate as a Jew, it would be realized in her descendants. It was tied up with the Land of Israel. It was a destiny that involved much suffering.

When Gilo, the southernmost neighborhood of Jerusalem, is sprayed nightly by machine-gun fire from Bait Jala, the roads are closed, stranding us in Jerusalem. Or the bus to Kiriat Arba goes by way of Bait Shemesh, so that getting home is an ordeal. I arrived home the other night at two in the morning; I count my blessings that I got home at all.

An Israeli woman from Gilo was shot in the neck as she stood on her porch watching the gun battles. She is in critical condition. Our army-wise children told us that the media doesn't report the hundreds of misses. Prime Minister Barak still wants the people to believe in his "peace."

Yossi, fearless, was driving a car without the double-plastic windows that protect against stones. These windows do not protect against bullets, but no one dares drive without them in Judea and Samaria. Yossi inherited his father's fearlessness and, like his father twelve years ago, came under a hail of stones not far from his home in Samaria.

The stones burst Yossi's tires and smashed his windshield. He was treated by army medics who removed pieces of glass from his face. Then he went home.

November 8

No end to the violence in sight. I think we are at war, not from an enemy without but from a people who have become an enemy within. A car bomb went off in the Mahane Yehuda Market on Thursday, the busiest day of the week. It killed a young mother, the daughter of National Religious party Knesset member, Yitzhak Levy, as she stood by the truck which had just brought furniture to her new apartment. Yair Levy, a lawyer on his way to buy a pita and felafel, was killed too.

A young Israeli soldier was killed near Bethlehem when his patrol was summoned there after shots had been fired at an Israeli car. Sharpshooters shot him in the head.

An army reserve soldier, father of a family, was killed near Jericho.

People turn to each other and ask, "What will be?"

But no one has an answer. This is odd in itself. Settlers used to be so sure they knew God's plans.

Nightly the Jewish neighborhoods of Hebron come under rifle fire from the Arab neighborhoods. Every time the shooting begins—the single fire of the Arabs, and the blasting back from our forces—I call Estie on her cellular phone. It rings and rings. I am frightened when she is unable to answer. I imagine dreadful things.

Last night Frank and I got into the car and drove down to Hebron. It is a very steep hill, almost a plunge from Kiriat Arba into the old city. The road, made for donkeys and carts, is narrowly hugged by old hovels made from the local stones, rising from the same-colored earth. It is also bordered by more modern Arab buildings made of the polished marble for which Hebron is famous, luminous in the night like ghosts.

Heaven for rats. Heaven for terrorists. The snaking asphalt drops us into the valley in which the city proper lies; the Cave of the Patriarchs and Matriarchs looms in the night. Around it, crumbling, are the ruins of ancient Jewish dwellings.

We are now entirely exposed to the mountainside Arab neighborhood of Abu Sneineh. Lately many of us have been shot at, so the Israeli army shuts off the street lamps at night so that Jewish movement cannot be seen. We turn off the headlights of the car and creep toward Bait Hadassah where we know Estie is manning an outpost.

Bait Hadassah, a three-story apartment building erected for Jewish settlers in the 1980s, took its name from the Hadassah

Clinic upon which it is built. The clinic had served the Jewish community until the pogrom of 1929.

Mixed in with the smell of medicines which amazingly still lingers there, are memories. There is the apartment of the pharmacist who, despite his wife's pleas not to, opened the door to his Arab neighbors believing they were truly in need of his help. In cruel and bizarre ways, they tortured, then murdered him and his family.

Outside Bait Hadassah, Israeli soldiers are now positioned. One of them is wearing fatigues that are too big for her and a helmet that completely shadows her face. Her rifle is hanging from her shoulder. It is almost as long as she is tall. She holds it loosely, one hand on the barrel, one hand on the trigger mechanism. It is Estie.

The quick smile she gives us vanishes just as quickly. "Are you crazy? Why did you come down here?"

I answer, "How can I let you be in the cross fire while I sit quietly at home?"

As we were talking, bullets started flying overhead. Arab gunmen were shooting, and our response, including red tracer bullets, looked like a moving stream of fireworks beneath the stars. Estie yelled at us to take cover.

"Not without you!" I tried to pull her after me, but she wrenched herself free. Frank put his arm around me, leading me quickly to shelter. The shelter happened to be the home of Anat Cohen, the famed Jewish fighter of Hebron.

Veteran of many street battles with Arabs and Israeli soldiers alike, she has been beaten up many times by Israeli police for her militant Zionism. She has been arrested countless times; she has been charged with aggression against Arabs. Once, she was targeted and then run over by an Arab car.

She is the mother of eleven. She is the daughter of the legendary Moshe Zar, who for years bought up land from Arabs to sell to Jews, until Arabs attacked him and tried to cut out his throat. Partially disabled by the attack, Anat's father, together with her mother, live in a villa they built on a mount in Samaria, the only proud and fearless Jews for miles around.

It was they who renovated the antiquated home where we now waited out Estie's gun battle. I was not in the mood for talking.

I listened to Anat. She told us that the Jewish children of Hebron have become experts in weaponry. They know from the sound of each blast what kind of guns the Arabs are using; the Kalachnikovs we gave them; the M-16s they stole; the heavy machine guns they smuggled in. In the morning the children collect spent cartridges, not only from the street but also from the floors of their living rooms and bedrooms. The Arabs shoot into their houses at night.

Anat said, "Do you know how God does miracles for us all the time? How many bullets pass over our heads and behind our backs and by our sides? Miracles. Miracles."

Across the gully where my children once played with Arab children, the Israeli army recaptured the hillock which had been ceded to the Palestinian Authority during one phase of the pullback under Barak. The Israeli flag now flies over the Arab school which the Arabs originally built with a larger purpose in mind. It was a fortress.

Now our tanks are dug in there. At night we can hear the firing of their cannons and mortars. I believe the war is escalating; we have never heard these things before.

Two nights ago the northernmost neighborhood of Kiriat Arba was attacked. Israeli armored personnel carriers were brought in and gunfire raged all night. Nobody on our side was injured, but in the morning some of my neighbors found their yards littered with dead birds that had been shot out of the trees.

I am no longer in a clear frame of mind. I am mindful only of bullets, hatred, fear, and not knowing.

The not knowing what will be. This will kill you if bullets won't.

November 23

My aunt keeps calling and telling me to get out of Kiriat Arba. Then she tells me she wants to let me in on a big secret. But it is not a big secret. I know.

My father, may his soul rest in peace, never really accepted the fact that we moved to Israel. My father, who knew only one word in Yiddish, once said to Frank, "I call that *chutzpah*, to bring your children to live in Hebron."

My aunt sighs. "You know June, of all the people in our

family, you were the one who could have made the most of yourself, but you pissed your life away in Israel."

"Pissed my life away?" She has hit me where it hurts. I have always had my doubts.

"Having raised five children doesn't mean anything?" I counter weakly.

"Well, you were doing so beautifully in New York City, living on the Bowery writing poetry."

"I haven't been writing?"

"Oh, that stuff! About all the killings? Who wants to read that?"

"But I've written other things too."

"Oh you try hard, but your thoughts in Israel are different than they would have been in America. Your sort of thoughts just won't make you successful.

"Why did you ever leave? You know your father never approved of that. You took his grandchildren away from him, the pleasure of watching them grow up."

I am just about to cut off the conversation when she says, "June, did your father leave you any money when he died?"

"Not a penny," I answered, and then I burst out crying.

Within three days alone, in Gush Qatif, five Israelis were killed and many injured. This particular spate of violence began on Friday when Arabs overtook an Israeli army position outside Kfar Drom and killed two soldiers.

On Monday a 120-mm mortar shell exploded just as two buses went by taking the children of Kfar Drom to school. Three children from one family, the Cohen family, lost their

42

limbs. Orit, twelve years old, had a foot amputated; Israel, ten years old, lost one leg; Tehilla, eight, lost both legs.

There is no other way to stay sane but to disconnect emotionally from the horrors. My children are doing that. My neighbors are doing that. That's why I'm writing these things down like a laundry list, shutting up my heart, trying not to go mad from the pain of imagining what it would be like to have one child so terribly injured and maimed. But three?

Noga, their mother, says she is sure that God loves her children and that he will help her take care of them and cope; for surely she and her husband cannot cope alone. They have four children at home who were not on the bus at the time, plus the three who once played, ran, swam, jumped, and hopped and are now amputees. What pain will they live with day in and day out for the rest of their lives?

Some say, "At least they have lives." Miriam Amitai, a teacher who was on the bus with them, was killed. Also killed was Gabi Biton. Together they leave a total of ten orphans in the besieged settlement of Kfar Drom. There, scarcely a single family knows what it's like to be whole and happy. There, many of the families are already missing mothers and fathers from earlier terrorist attacks.

The next morning, when Ittamar, an eighteen-year-old boy from a nearby settlement, came to help the people of Kfar Drom put up a security fence, Arab snipers shot off his head.

November 27

Shmulik just finished his military service. After four and a half years in submarines, he needs pure air. He needs space in which to breathe and move freely, a mental space not crowded or clouded with terrorism. He packed up his backpack and will set off for America to visit relatives for the first time since he immigrated with us when he was almost two. He wants to see what we left. He wants to understand why we left.

After a few months he will go to South America. He'll be gone a year, and though I will miss him terribly, I'm glad for now that he will be there and not here.

"It's against the Torah to leave Israel unless it's for business or to visit family," say the religious Zionist children in my family.

Frank argues with them. "Then our God is just a local deity like the god of a Japanese mountain."

"No," our religious children answer. "Our God is God of everything and every country. But he loves Israel best, so this is where he wants the Chosen People to live. Do you want to be somewhere where God doesn't want you to be?"

We took Shmulik to the airport this afternoon. He made me promise I wouldn't cry like I had the day he was drafted into the navy. We all hugged him goodbye, and as he walked through the departure gate he kept turning back to make sure I was keeping my word.

Only when the automatic doors finally shut did I break my promise.

In Samaria, settlers, including my son Yossi, have been issued bulletproof vests which they put on before traveling. These vests can protect only their chests and backs against bullets. Nothing can be done to protect their necks and heads.

In Judea, where we live, *all* buses have now been made bulletproof. In Gush Qatif, in the Gaza Strip, civilian vehicles are no longer allowed to travel the roads. The people who live there travel in convoys of armored vehicles which leave at designated times each day. A friend of mine who had just come back from there told me a story.

Miriam Amitai's daughter, orphaned last month when the bus her mother was riding in drove over an explosive device, was riding the bus once again, this time an armored one. Talking to a friend who wanted something from her, the daughter said in a sing-song voice, "I can't give it to you, my mother won't let me, ha ha. I just said that. I'm kidding. I don't have a mother."

"So what?" the friend shot back. "I don't have a father."

December 8

At 7:30 in the morning, Yossi called. These days the phone often rings at that hour; it's always a friend or family member with bad news. My heart went from its usual place into my mouth.

"Where is Aba?" he asked me.

I told him he had left for Tel Aviv. "Why?"

Yossi said there had been a terrorist attack a few minutes earlier outside the gate of Kiriat Arba. "Two people are dead," he said.

My hand began to shake. "Who?"

"I don't know. I'll make a few phone calls." Yossi works in security and could quickly find out the names of those murdered.

At the same time Yossi received the message about the attack, Haim Didovski, who lives at the settlement of Bait Haggai and runs a news service, got a message on his beeper—the two people killed had been in a white pickup truck, a man and a woman. He knew that his wife Rina was on her way to the Kiriat Arba Religious Elementary School to teach her fourth-grade class. She was in a white pickup truck. He called her cellular phone. She didn't answer.

Rina, mother of six, had one clean bullet hole through her head. So deadly was the bullet, she simply slumped onto her friend, a fellow schoolteacher, without uttering a word. Then her mobile phone rang.

Murdered with her was Eliahu ben Ami, the driver. So big, so strong, so confident, he was the pride of his four children. They felt he was like Samson—no bullet, no bomb, nothing could ever cut him down.

When will this all end? We're all so tired, God. Please protect me and my family. Don't allow my children to be orphaned. Don't let me be widowed. Don't let us be maimed.

I see the Cohen children lying in the hospital without their legs. At night I see the head of Rina slumped over her briefcase containing homework assignments covered with blood. I hear the principal of the school calling two of her young daughters into his office. When they sit down, he says, "There was a terrorist attack outside of Kiriat Arba."

"We know," they said.

"Your mother was killed."

Friends coming from the *shivah* where Rina's family sit in mourning say that Haim, her husband, cries that he's an orphan too. Rina held their lives together. Rina's baby son, I understand, still nurses. On Friday night Rina's family ate the Sabbath food she had prepared before she was killed.

Shmulik is on Cape Cod, just two hundred miles from our first homestead in Massachusetts. He says the landscape is indescribable. He has never seen such a pretty thing in his life. He asks how we can get along in such a little place as Israel (especially in a settlement) even in times of peace.

But now? How is it humanly possibly to live there? What is keeping us rooted to Kiriat Arba and Hebron? He has not yet found answers to these questions. Everything we left behind looks so polished and bright.

He worries about us. I tell him to get it out of his mind. There'll be plenty of time for him to worry when he gets back.

December 14

We pulled out of Lebanon. Now we have Lebanon here. The stepped-up Intifada has turned into a war waged against men, women, children, and soldiers. Whoever is Israeli is a legitimate target for Arab gunmen.

I do not use the words "Arab terrorists." There is no clear distinction anymore between the civilian Arab population and the terrorists. I just heard that the General Security Services (GSS) picked up the Arab suspected of murdering Rina and Eliahu. He is a vendor in the market in Hebron. After he drove by and shot them up, he went to sell tomatoes.

In the past few weeks on the bypass road to Jericho, Arabs killed two soldiers, one on a bus traveling from Tiberias to Jerusalem, a route no one ever worried about before.

In Samaria a civilian working for the Israeli army was killed. A "civilian"? What an empty word for a person agonizingly missed by a mother and a father, wife and children longing for him forever. Each person killed is a world.

Many others were lightly injured when they were ambushed. "Lightly injured"? do those words conjure up the damage done to the texture of interwoven lives?

There have been several car bombings and suicide bombers that I haven't even written about. I can't keep up with them all. Nor do I want to. The situation is out of control. Gory and grizzly, it is our fare from day to day. We try not to think about it. We try to bury our heads in blessed daily routine—blessed because we know how fragile, how finite, and short-lived it may be.

Prime Minister Ehud Barak has resigned, calling for early elections which will take place within two months. Most of the Israeli leftists that Frank and I know say they will now vote for Netanyhu, who will most probably run.

They admit they made a catastrophic mistake when they supplied the Arabs with weapons as part of a peace treaty. They confess to having erred in freeing hundreds of Arab terrorists from Israeli prisons, as stipulated in the peace accords. They admit it was a mistake to funnel millions upon millions of dollars into Arafat's bank account, and to continue to do so in spite of the Intifada. They acknowledge that they created a monster who rules over autonomous areas into which the army may not pursue an attacker.

Even Frank and I, thought of as being soft on Arabs by our religious Zionist settler neighbors, have been driven far to the political right.

So the country, torn by grief and fear, is uniting. The question is, will we still have a country to be united within? There is a proposal for a "Bypass Israel" road. It will go directly into the sea.

January 1, 2001

What madness! Barak, on his way out as prime minister, has just returned from Washington after conferring with President Clinton, on his way out too. As a last-ditch effort to go down in history as the men who brought peace to the Middle East, these two lame ducks have offered half of Israel to Arafat!

Is our prime minister planning mass suicide for us, a final solution to our problem? Or are we like the lemmings, those psychotic animals that every so often rush maddeningly in droves into the sea?

In addition to ceding 95 percent of Judea and Samaria, all of the Gaza Strip, some of the desert north of Eliat, and some of the Jordan Valley to Arafat, Barak says he is now willing to negotiate the future of East Jerusalem and the Temple Mount.

No previous Israeli government has been willing to discuss dividing Jerusalem into east and west. Jerusalem undivided, they said, is the capital of the Jewish nation for eternity. And the cornerstone of that capital is the Temple Mount; and the Temple Mount is in East Jerusalem.

Oddly, a rabbinical decree forbids Jews from going up to the Temple Mount, and not because it is in East Jerusalem. The rabbis reason that since the ashes of the red heifer were destroyed with King Solomon's Temple almost two thousand years ago, Jews do not possess the means to purify themselves. Therefore we are all in a state of impurity.

Jews, they say, must content themselves to pray at the Western or Wailing Wall, which is actually only a fragment of an outer wall of the Mount. Weep there and pray there, they say, for Jews cannot go to the holiest place on earth.

It was the Creator of the Universe himself, the rabbis say, citing the Bible, who directed King Solomon to build the First Temple for the Israelite nation. The peak of Mt. Moriah was removed, and in its place a man-made mount was fashioned and covered with smooth stone slabs. Upon this supernatural plateau the Temple, stark in its geometric forms, was built.

The Mount itself is all that remains of the Israelite glory. Around the Mount, Arab hustlers now work; it is their turf. Every minute another tour guide followed us around offering his services.

In the unearthly expanse before the Temple Mount, Muslim children play; they toss rocks at walls and circle on their bicycles. Muslim families picnic together to the hum of Arab work crews.

The Waqf (the Islamic Religious Trust) has been digging a tunnel connecting the mosques on the Mount. There is a stone-cutting machine, heavy building tools, and scaffolding.

But since stage two of the Intifada broke out, the Waqf has forbidden all Jews to go up to the Mount, including the Israeli Antiquities Authorities who are concerned that the excavations are destroying precious archaeological remains of the Holy Temple.

But before stage two, not accepting the rabbinical decree, Frank and I ascended the steps of the Temple Mount. Where the innermost sanctuary of the Temple once stood and God's presence once dwelled, the gold Dome of the Rock mosque stands. It commands all eyes and hearts in Jerusalem to behold that it is the Muslims who rule there now.

Frank touched my arm. "Do you feel it? That strong wind?" A powerful pulse reminded him of the flapping of wings against his chest.

I said no. It was a hot day, and not a stream of air moved.

He said, "Now I understand why people believe that angels have wings."

Shmulik says that America is rich in any way you look at it. Nature. Economics. Food to infinity. People are relaxed. When they leave the house in the morning they don't worry that they may come back in body bags.

He is starting to think like our relatives there. He said that Frank and I must leave Kiriat Arba. We have no interest in being settlers anymore. We should let the young ones do the job. We put in our time for the Zionist dream. Our dream should now be to have a good and interesting time.

"But don't be ashamed of the hard life we've had in Israel. You made the right choice, and I'm happy we grew up there. It was a perfect childhood for us, really."

Miriam said that at school her friends are busy writing their own eulogies.

A few weeks ago a friend said to her, "I'm not going to go to Rina's funeral today. I'll go to whoever's funeral there is tomorrow."

Are we numbed? Cynical? Whatever happened to the fresh optimism of Israelis that I found so repulsive?

Hours after a terrorist victim had been laid to rest, *yeshiva* boys would dance in the streets singing, "The Children of Israel Will Return."

They were sure that each pain was a sign that the Redemption was only closer at hand. They would quote from great rabbis who said that in the days of the coming of the Messiah, life would be so painful that they wouldn't want to be there to witness his coming.

Why aren't they singing now? After all, Rabbi Binyamin Ze'ev Kahane and his wife Talia were buried hours ago.

They were killed at 6:40 a.m. yesterday as they drove with a van load of their children near the settlement of Ofra. They thought that by leaving their home early they would be safer. But Binyamin Ze'ev got a bullet in his neck. Losing control of the car, he drove his family off the road into a *wadi*, leaving behind a trail of toys and books, one for prayer, and one about the happiness of the Jewish home. He and his wife leave behind five orphans, some of them injured too.

Binyamin Ze'ev was the son of Rabbi Meir Kahane, assassinated in New York in 1990. Meir Kahane founded the Jewish Defense League and later the militant Kach party in Israel. When Kach came out in favor of Baruch Goldstein's massacre of Arabs, the Kach party was condemned as a terrorist organization and outlawed. Binyamin Ze'ev then established his party, Kahane Lives.

Talia Kahane was the daughter of an American immigrant who tried to live as he believed our forefathers did. When we first came to Israel and were living in Tiberias, we met him. Frank would occasionally help him pasture his flocks on the hills of Galilee. Talia was nine years old then. Now she is dead at the age of thirty-two.

The escalation of the terror is Yasir Arafat's shocking response to Barak's peace offering of most of Israel.

The chairman of the Palestinian Authority says that Barak's offering does not contain the "right of return." This right would enable all Arab refugees who fled from Israel during past wars to return. As there are four million of them, the "right of return" would effectively change Israel from a Jewish country to an Arab one.

"What will be?" Menasseh Kam, who used to be a grocer here, asked me. He is the father of many children. One of them has a steel plate in her head from the time thirteen years ago when the little school bus she was in was stoned.

"What will be?" I do not know. There are no prophets around these days, though we are in great and dire need.

Menasseh is talking. He reminds me that every time an Israeli prime minister made plans to give up sovereignty over especially holy places in Israel—Hebron, Shechem, and any part of Jerusalem—that prime minister fell.

"Menachem Begin into serious illness and depression. Yitzhak Rabin by the bullet of Yigal Amir. Barak now. The Arabs are God's instruments.

"Just like God hardened the heart of Pharaoh, God is hardening the heart of Arafat. Barak offered him half of Israel, and he refused!

"This hardening of his heart will make the peace fall apart

so Barak won't get reelected. God will never let us give up this land."

Gadi Maresha is dead of bullet wounds. Gadi was a thirty-year-old resident of Kiriat Arba who immigrated from Ethiopia in 1981. He was just a boy during Operation Moshe, when the Ethiopians were brought out *en masse* from the Sudan.

They made the perilous journey from Ethiopia to the Sudan on foot. Many died on the way of starvation, of thirst, of violent attacks by bandits, but they went on, certain that the Messiah had come and was waiting for them in the Sudan with silver wings that would bear them back to their Jerusalem of gold.

Gadi was a career officer. His parents were so proud of him. A bomb went off in Gush Qatif, killing both Gadi and the soldier with him, Yonathan Vermullen, a Christian immigrant who had given up his country to live in the Holy Land.

My seventeen-year-old Yehoshua went to some of the funerals. Our children are burying their dead. Where I was brought up, in America, children didn't know anyone who had died. I was unusual in that respect.

January 7

Shmulik left America for Ecuador. As much as he loved America, he came to an important conclusion. "My country is Israel. All the wonderful things I saw made me realize that it is our job to create a good country in spite of its smallness, in spite of all its weaknesses. We have a lot to learn from the Americans. Oh, America may be more beautiful and more peaceably located. But God gave us the land of Israel in the heart of the Middle East."

Who was murdered this week or only critically injured? A study should be conducted on the mental state of most of us. Yehoshua sat down at the computer and wrote, "It is good to die for your country."

"No," I cried. "It is good to *live* for your country. Enough death. Enough! Live! *Want* to live. It is not good to die."

January 28

Yossi is a father! Adi had a baby! Frank and I are grandparents!

A little girl. Her name is Shachar Malchut, which means Dawn and the Kingdom. It is a Messianic name, of course.

Many say we are now living the agonizing War of Gog and Magog, a war to usher in the days of the Messiah. The Messiah will be a great ruler, a descendant of King David who will rebuild the Third Holy Temple, which will never be destroyed.

And in Jerusalem the priestly caste, the Cohens, will put on their sacred vestments with twelve stones on the breastplate, one for each tribe. Every Jew will pass before them, and the stone that supernaturally lights up will indicate the lost tribe from which he came. There will be Jews who will find out they are not Jews at all; there will be gentiles who will discover they are Jews.

Then all true Jews will purify themselves with the ashes of the red heifer and bring sacrifices once again to the Holy Temple. Torah will waft out of Jerusalem and fill the whole world. Prophecy will be renewed. The Gentiles will come to speak with the prophets and offer their sacrifices to God who has once again found a dwelling place in this world.

The rocks will be so joyous that they will talk to us; the trees will yield their secrets. And after the Messiah has led us in a holy war to establish our true and God-given borders, we will beat our rifles into plowshares.

Then the lion will lie down with the lamb, and the art of war will be forgotten. Each person will sit under his own fig tree contemplating the beauties of the Kingdom.

My granddaughter's name means "We are in the dawn" of this Kingdom of Israel which will never perish or become corrupt again. The final kingdom which will never fall.

Shachar Malchut is a member of the second generation of Leavitts to live in the Land of Israel, the beginning of an answer to my prayer. Perhaps there was a reason why we came to Israel. Maybe we will put down roots from which will grow a tree that is sound and healthy and not scarred and bent by ancestral memories.

For in the kingdom there is a house. It is my house. How

I've meditated that we will see blessings in it—grandchildren, great-grandchildren, and many marriages.

And my meditations have been answered. How much happier I am than my mother, who never even saw her own children grow up.

When I approached the age of forty, I was frightened that my life would be cut off like hers, like her brother's, like her father's. Her grandfather also died at forty, killed by a train a few days after he immigrated to America—the karma of *mazel*, the Yiddish word for luck.

How I prayed that coming to Israel and surviving would break that curse at last. And here we are with a new scion, strong, making roots, growing.

February 2

Arieh Hershkowitz, the man who gave Yossi and Adi a beautiful wooden table when they married, was killed as he drove home to Ofra.

Leor Atiah was murdered in Jenin when he picked up his car at the Arab garage.

Dr. Shmuel Gellis, a brilliant doctor at Hadassah, was killed not far from his home just after calling his wife on his cell phone to tell her he would be home within minutes. A car parked by the side of the road, blinkers flashing as if stuck, pulled out as Shmuel Gellis passed, and then sped by him. Trained Arab gunmen sprayed bullets through the double Plexiglas window and emptied their guns into his neck and head. He wore a bullet-proof vest which protected only his torso.

Yes, the Arabs have superbly trained gunmen and armor-piercing bullets that can penetrate even certain bulletproof vests. Whatever we do, they will seek to penetrate our attempts to stay alive.

The Barak government has fallen. Clinton is out too, but the damage they did lives on. Maybe Clinton is more to blame. With his charisma, power, and charm, and the reserves of the American Treasury, he coerced Barak, and Rabin before him, to create a "Palestine" in our midst that is powerfully armed and lethal. And he did this under the banner of peace.

Just as in the story of "The Emperor's New Clothes," when dishonest tailors made robes of nothing, the Israeli left cried out how beautiful the new peace agreement was.

Election day is Tuesday. Ariel Sharon, not Binyamin Netanyahu, is running against Ehud Barak. Ariel Sharon also knows the story of the emperor's new clothes.

In Hebron, Estie is caught once again between the hammer and the anvil—Arabs shooting at her position, settlers trying to push past her into the autonomous area where the Arab gunfire originates.

Though Miriam promised never *ever* to come to Hebron to demonstrate as long as Estie served there, she said she couldn't stand the situation any longer.

"Get out of here before I smash you with this!" Estie pushed the settlers back with the butt end of her rifle.

Miriam cried. "Why are you on their side? Why are you going to let the Arabs kill us?"

"Traitor!" other settlers screamed at Estie.

A woman soldier grabbed Miriam's arm. Miriam resisted. When the soldier raised her arm to hit Miriam, Estie screamed, "Don't touch her! She's my sister!"

"Just whose side are you on?" her comrade-in-arms shouted back.

February 10

Three days after Frank left for Japan, only now I sit down to write. I write not in order to soothe my misery or panic but to say that yoga has given me great strength.

I was afraid to do a handstand. Trying to do one, I felt my fear to be like a physical, sticky substance that had to be dissolved, a fear that symbolized all other fears. Step by step I learned to kick up into a handstand without feeling what supported me—not seeing it but trusting it was there.

Like living here. Trusting it is there—an invisible and invincible thread which carries the meaning of my life from the womb of my mother and the seed of my father, son of German-Jewish immigrants who settled in Washington Heights.

After eight months of trying, I kicked up into a handstand. I was there. "There" was a simple effortless place, the place of no fear.

"No fear" follows me through every day. It followed me yesterday when I drove Miriam on roads I never dared before. These days most people don't drive on these roads.

Where did I get such coolness and calm? Now that these qualities are with me, I never want them to leave. What did I do right? If I knew, I would do that right thing over and over again.

Is it the yoga or is it arriving at the age of fifty, when all passions, including fear, are calmed and cooled?

So this is what my husband calls faith! The ingredient without which you cannot live in Israel.

I think of verses from Buddhist scripture and know that they are true.

By faith the flood is crossed!
By wakefulness the sea.
By vigor ill is passed
By wisdom cleansed is he.

Ariel Sharon is the new prime minister. His right-wing position (which the world hates) might give us the confidence to believe that when we leave the house we will return home alive and whole.

His wife Lilly died just months ago. Who will give him the strength to govern this unruly nation? To whom will he come home after each grueling day? Who will help him make the decisions on which the fate of his people depends?

Now begins the difficult work of putting a government together. Sharon may have to include ultra-Orthodox Jews (who are not Zionists) as well as the Labor party that created the "peace" and havoc we are in today.

February 16

Sunday night, on the road between the two tunnels on the Jerusalem-Hebron highway, Zacky Sassoon, father of two, was killed as he drove home. The bullets fired from Bait Jala pierced his windshield, and Zacky crashed into the retaining wall. Huey Cobra helicopters had to hover over the road when the ambulance that had been rushed in to save him came under fire. He died at Hadassah Hospital. His wife, an American immigrant, said that she had had terrible premonitions all week. Zacky told her they were nonsense.

Wednesday morning at 8 a.m., an Arab bus driver for Egged, the Israeli bus cooperative, dropped off workers from Gaza then plowed into a bus stop crowded with soldiers, instantly killing nine young men and women and injuring twenty-two. He then sped away. The police chased after him and shot out his tires.

I think of yoga. I began studying it in New York at the age of twenty-two when I went to live on the Bowery in New York City.

In meditative breathing, the body has a tendency to collapse when air is exhaled. The lungs deflate; air leaves the body and carries the *prana* or life force with it. And against this tendency to deflate, we try to keep the torso strong and upright.

That's what I am trying to do when I think of Shivi Keller being shot in the legs as he drove on the Beer Sheba–Kiriat Arba road yesterday evening, the same road Frank drives morning and night. I'm trying not to deflate.

They say he is in the hospital screaming in pain, "God! God! I know you are all goodness! I know I deserve this, but please help! Help me God!"

Shivi Keller? He is tall and wild-eyed with a glass eye replacing the real one he lost when a stone went through his windshield during stage one of the Intifada.

There are some who live here whose very presence gives you a shot of energy, renewed faith. Yair Har Sinai, the shepherd, is one of them. He still pastures his flocks out in the Hebron Hills every day.

Shivi is one of them too, in his billowy white cottons and his *tallith*, his ritual prayer shawl. Three years ago he frightened away a group of Arab shepherds who began stoning him out in a lonely field where he had gone to commune with God. By doing somersaults and crying "Shema Yisrael!" the Arabs, thinking he was *majnun*, crazy, left him alone.

The Arabs have an uncanny sense of whom to hit—those special ones who give us confidence, pride, and a sense of power. Shivi is a musician who writes melodies to accompany the Psalms of David. He puts out CDs about faith in God and Israel that my religious daughter Miriam loves to dance to.

Shivi played the bongo drums at Yossi's wedding, and everyone danced to his rhythms. Now the thighs that held the drums are shattered. The spinning bullets that were used against him spiraled through bone, cartilage, and nerves.

His wife is expecting her sixth baby any day. Miriam has gone over to their house to see if she can help.

March 12

Living here teaches you to be grateful for small things. One more flood crossed. One more ill passed.

Estie has been transferred out of Hebron. As strong as she is, she was cracking in the middle—tormented on one side by friends, neighbors, and her sister, and on the other by Arabs shooting guns. She would come home enraged.

Her last post in Hebron was at the 160 junction, a post set up after a van taking nursery school teachers from Kiriat Arba into Hebron was shot at from a rooftop there. On that occasion, our neighbor Fanny Eliezer got a bullet in her throat.

Estie and two other soldiers manned the junction from a pile of stone rubble. Bringing her pita and hummus one night, I was shocked to see not only the danger of where she stood but the filth. Because of all the unrest, the Palestinian Authority had not been taking away the garbage. Rats were everywhere! Is this the same Estie who loves to work at clothing stores and spend all her money on liquid-tight pants? She wanted to be a combat soldier. She saw only the glory.

We do not make the consequences, we only make the blind decisions. And so we learn.

April 24

I will not write about Shalhevet Pas, the ten-month-old infant who was shot dead in Hebron while her parents pushed her in her stroller toward the neighborhood of Avraham Avinu to visit her grandparents. The Arab sniper looked through the barrel of his rifle from the neighborhood of Abu Sneineh, and pulled the trigger when he saw her cranium in his cross hairs.

On the seventh day of mourning, the day of a memorial ceremony at her fresh little grave, Iska Levinger was about to drive up to the cemetery when she realized that her children's faces were full of chocolate. As she leaned into the trunk of her car to get "Wipies," something hot hit her cheek. Thankfully, the bullet just grazed her.

Nor will I write at length of the violence and unrest which has worsened in Hebron since Estie was transferred north. Scores of settlers, Miriam among them, keep trying to get past army blockades in order to take over Abu Sneineh. They say that Ariel Sharon is worse than Barak and as bad as Rabin. They voted for right-wing Sharon, but he then set up a National Unity government in which Shimon Peres, the engineer of the peace process, occupies a key cabinet post. Peres belongs to the Labor party, the old power base of this country. The settlers contend that he is really running the show.

The new minister of defense, Binyamin Ben-Eliezer, is also entrenched in the old power elite. The elections changed nothing.

Abu Sneineh must be reconquered. There are signs everywhere showing Shalhevet's picture, saying that her blood cries out for revenge. "TAKE ABU SNEINEH NOW."

I don't have the energy to write now. I've been laid low for the past month. Acute bronchitis. I tried to keep my torso strong and upright, but it deflated after all. I'm very scared.

I think of my friend Tzviah Blumethal who is battling a melanoma which has spread throughout her body. Her husband Yisrael cares for her lovingly. I am thinking of the Cohen children without legs, and Shivi full of metal, struggling in pain to walk on steel crutches; of Shelhevet's young mother, and her father who was injured in the same attack; of all the people who have been killed just this year alone.

And I was thinking about what a rabbi, immersed in the Kabala, once said. There will be a purge. Half the Jewish nation will be wiped out before the Messiah comes.

I took the Bach Flower Remedies—similar to homeopathic essences—for thoughts that keep torturing me. I took them for my fears and for strength when I didn't have a drop of it left. I took them for thinking that I can't go on, for regretting that Frank and I made our fateful decision to come to Israel.

Maybe, just maybe you exercise free will when you first make a decision. But afterward, all that follows is disconnected from your willing it or not. It comes throttling out from somewhere and carries you along in its momentum.

All you can say is, "No, this is not what I meant. This is not what I meant at all."

May 2

As if to herald strange and terrible things, the sky was yellow all over Israel on Monday. It burst into furious gales of hot wind, dropping torrents of hail and balls of rain.

Then Asaf Hershkowitz, who lost his father Arieh three months ago in a drive-by shooting near Ofra, was killed on the same road, in almost the same place, and in the same way as his father. Arabs drove by pumping a magazine of bullets into him. Thirty years old, he was the father of two.

I was supposed to go to yoga class. But I lay in bed trying to separate myself from the madness that has become so awful that my yoga teacher told me her dog scratched and whined all night. I could barely sleep either. Then, during the dark dawn, the sky let loose again, and I could not move from bed.

Maybe in the stillness I will sense the meaning of it all, a pattern in the pain.

Families are breaking up. Bodies are breaking up. Heads are breaking up, both literally and figuratively. Pain seeps into the marrow of the people here, people who always maintained their faith and cheer no matter what.

With the signing of the accords and agreements that would weaken Israel strategically, suddenly this country had money it never seemed to have before. Beginning in the late 1980s, modern cars, vans, mini-buses, and four-wheel drives from America and Japan began to fill the ports. Readily available loans backed by American money made it possible for many Israelis to buy these vehicles.

Moving out of modest apartments, many Israelis settled into custom-built palatial villas. They put big color televisions in each room, where not long ago there was only one black-and-white television per block, which families would gather around. They put in cable so they could receive American programs, and bought state-of-the-art stereo systems to hear Madonna and American rock groups while they ate McDonald's hamburgers and fries.

The price extracted for this gust of affluence was territorial—"concessions." For nonreligious Israelis who do not believe in divine claims to any piece of earth, the price they negotiated seemed more than fair. For the many religious Zionists who just as zealously built beautiful homes, confusion crept into their lives.

Religious Zionists are followers of the late chief rabbi of Israel, Rabbi Kook. There had always been among them a mystical glorification of the modern state of Israel. Wasn't the establishment of the state of Israel the first sign of Messianic days? Wasn't the Holy Temple to be rebuilt soon, never to be destroyed again?

Isn't the steady flow of Jewish returnees the fulfillment of God's promise to bring His Chosen from all corners of the earth after nearly two thousand years of exile?

To religious Zionists the state of Israel was synonymous with the biblical kingdom of Israel. And as the kingdom had been then, the state should now be the revelation of godliness in the world!

To become a soldier was the dream of every boy here. The settlers and their sons were the most highly motivated. They saw the Israeli Defense Forces as a rebirth of the biblical army of the children of Israel. Male settlers always became combat soldiers and, quite frequently, officers in Israel's most elite units.

Unbelievably, now a number of settlers' children have become draft dodgers. People here don't like the government any more. They suspect that those who negotiated the peace are not really Jews but are the reincarnated souls of Gentiles who came out of Egypt with the Jews. The Kabala says that these souls of the "mixed multitude" will have us by our throats in the days that precede the Messiah.

Even disillusionment, at first intensely felt, turns into apathy. How can we stand up against the passion of Islam unless we are equally impassioned? Arabs blow themselves up as they quote the Koran.

And we? Are we going out with a whimper, beaten into semi-consciousness by money and a zealous foe?

May 8

We are burying another of our dead. This time it was a natural death, if dropping dead at fifty-three can be called a natural death. Chaim Magany and his wife Shoshana, both fiery religious Zionists from America, were among the first Jews to resettle Hebron after the Six-Day War. They have lived here ever since. His name used to be Beshitz, but he chose a Hebrew name instead. Mageny means "my shield."

Chaim died of heart failure on Friday. Neighbors say he took the situation too much to heart. He was a tour guide and was having trouble making a living because of the Intifada. He was buried next to his parents in Hebron. He leaves behind eleven children.

Orphans. Orphans everywhere.

Arieh Orlanda was murdered in the middle of the night, not far from where Yossi's wife and baby lay sleeping. He was on guard duty near Ittamar when the Muslims stole up on him as he got out of his car to investigate a noise. They shot him, then stabbed him repeatedly. An army patrol found him and telephoned Yossi. With all of Yossi's training in resuscitation, there was nothing he could do.

Arieh is survived by a wife and two children.

May 29

Israel is swallowing up her people.

A huge banquet hall in Jerusalem collapsed during a wedding on Wednesday night. Twenty-three people were killed including Terefet Hamanrot, a girl we knew when we lived in the Sinai. She used to play with Shmulik on the sand dunes.

Israel is killing off her people like flies.

Anat Cohen's brother, Gilad Zar, seriously wounded by Arab gunfire two months ago, recuperated so quickly that he amazed the doctors and nurses at the hospital. Never had they seen anyone with such severe chest wounds get on his feet and back to a normal life in only six weeks.

At 7 a.m. an Arab car parked by the side of the road overtook Gilad's car. Sixty bullets came flying out the window at point-blank range. This time no miracle saved Gilad. He leaves behind a widow, eight children, and parents who fearlessly live alone on a mountaintop in Samaria.

Gilad was in charge of security for the whole Ittamar area and was Yossi's boss. His wife Hagar decorates for weddings. When Yossi and Adi married, she turned the barn into something beautiful. She hung beautiful sheets on the walls and put ceramic urns full of wheat and dried flowers all around the room. She has eight children whose broken lives she must make into something beautiful now.

Is this just one day? The Lubavitch rebbe once said that there is no contradiction between the biblical account of Creation and geological evidence that the world is millions of years old. If the events in those seven days were cataclysmic, he said, rocks would naturally show signs that millions of years had passed.

At 3 p.m. this afternoon Miriam went to the hitchhiking post in Kiriat Arba to flag down a ride to Jerusalem. A half-hour later Yossi called. He wanted to know where Miriam was. On the Kiriat Arba–Jerusalem road, one person had just been killed and another mortally injured. One of them was a teenage girl.

I told him that Miriam was on her way to Jerusalem in a

car. He said he was going to drive right away from Jerusalem to Gush Etzion where it happened. He had to find out if one of the slain victims was Miriam.

I took the Bach Flower Remedy for shock and waited.

Yossi sped there. Yehoshua sped there too. Yossi got there in time to lift the shroud that covered the dead body before the burial society took it away.

It was a well-groomed woman in brand-new running shoes. She looked American. He didn't recognize her face but was told that her name was Blaustein. She and her husband had immigrated to the wealthy Anglo-Saxon settlement of Efrat just months ago.

Today, in Efrat, she and her husband picked up a girl hitchhiking. Mrs. Blaustein told the girl that they were going to the funeral of Gilad Zar. The girl said she was going too.

The two of them ended up going to their own funerals instead—the young hitchhiker died on her way to the hospital.

Neither of them were Miriam. Relief? The quickness of life here moves us on in its stream.

The buses that took the people here to Gilad Zar's funeral afterward took them to the wedding of a seventeen-year-old girl from Hebron who was married this evening in Jerusalem. From funerals to weddings, anguish to joy, wailing to dancing, all in one day.

So much is compressed into each day that scientists in the future, examining our remains, will conclude that our lives spanned a millennium.

July 3

It cannot be. Such things cannot be.

Yair Har Sinai, the shepherd who gave us so much strength, continued to wander the hills of Hebron with his flocks even after Dov was killed, after Shivi was shot in the legs.

Without fear. Why should he fear? We knew that a heavenly host watched over him.

But the flock came back without the shepherd. Seeing the flock return without her husband, Dalia Har Sinai called security at Sussiya in the Hebron Hills where she lives.

Yossi got the message that Yair Har Sinai was missing. He called Yehoshua on his cellular phone. At one in the morning, when I heard Yehoshua stirring about, I got up and asked what he was doing. He mumbled something about a cookout. I was too sleepy to be suspicious.

He and his friend Uriel, whose mother just died from melanoma, weren't going to a cookout. They were on their way to Sussiya, twelve miles from here, to help in the search for Yair.

It was Yehoshua and Uriel who found Yair, his fingers grasping his *tallith* as if he had seen his assailants raise their guns and had tried to secure it. Yehoshua was sure he was in the middle of saying "Shema Yisrael. The Lord Our God. The Lord is One."

Yair had no gun, no knife. Harmony and a powerful faith flowed from him. He did everything like the Patriarchs, his wife Dalia like the Matriarchs. She is a beautiful, glowing, flowing woman who kneads her own organic bread, sells loaves, makes and sells natural cheeses. She and Yair are vegetarians. Peace-loving, they live with their nine children in the home they built with their own hands. There are no fences between them and the Arabs of Yatta. They were the envy of all of us for their pristine and spiritual ways.

We were all so sure angels watched over him. But angels keep no one alive these days. Yair was laid to rest next to Dov at 3 p.m. yesterday at the Sussiya Cemetery.

Jews in Israel today can do everything like the Patriarchs did except reach a ripe old age.

Spirituality does not protect one here. Powerful energy and vibrations do not protect one here. Good karma does not protect one here. Being beautiful in spirit and body does not protect one here. God protect us and watch over us!

Sometimes I believe that life is comprised of infinite possibilities; when we choose one, others seal off behind us. Each time we say "yes" we proliferate the "no's." There are many more paths we cannot follow than paths we can. It saddens me to think this way.

Frank knows exactly why I'm thinking this. He says, "No. There are *not* infinite possibilities. Had you gone any other way, you would not be you. You could only have come the way you came."

To Israel.

The cause of my coming to Israel is rooted in a time when I had no consciousness of being Jewish; when I hadn't even heard of the Six-Day War which I now know broke out on my birthday. It originated in my decision to attend a college which was ideologically distant from the American dream of material success.

I entered the University of Wisconsin wanting to be a journalist. When I left I was an eccentric would-be poet.

If I had attended another school, I am sure I would have pursued a respectable career in journalism, had few cares about money, and no dark thoughts about the murders of my friends. I would not have brought my children up to see death so closely that they can smell it, touch it, and see it behind their eyes at night. I might have provided them with a more secure future rather than a tragic ideal. That only in the land of Israel can a Jew be a Jew, and a Jew be proud. That only here does a Jew have roots. That only here can a Jew bloom and bear fruit, fruit that will be sweet for all mankind.

I chose to go to a university far away from Long Island, a university which, unknown to me, was a hotbed of radicalism. It was the center of the anti-Vietnam War movement which was a movement not only against the war. It was a movement against the entire American culture.

On my second day at the university when I showed up at the Rat Cellar where I heard the liberal arts students hung out, I was wearing a grey suede skirt with a matching vest and grey leather heels pulled out of my trousseau. I had applied a line of white on my eyelids, and then heavily coated my lashes with mascara.

"Hey, take a look at that Jewish princess!"

Catcalls, shrieks, laughing. Until I felt myself hot and red all over, I hadn't noticed that all the students in the smoky room were wearing jeans and tee shirts. Most of them were barefoot. All of them, boys and girls alike, had uncut, unruly hair.

"Hey Jewish princess, still a virgin? Saving it for Prince Charming?"

I went back to the dorm dejected and confused. Weren't girls supposed to dress to kill? If I wasn't supposed to do that, what was I supposed to do?

I reasoned that I might be happier if I socialized with the "straights." So I bought a season's pass for the football games. I went to my first game where I sat in the bleachers cheering and feeling miserable. The game was a bore. It was cold outside.

I bought myself a pair of blue jeans. I let my hair grow out of the neat and parted cut that framed my jaw, let it hang out loose and long. I went to class and learned things that turned the thoughts under my hair around. Marx taught me that I had formed wrong ideas about myself and what I ought to be. Now I wanted to be liberated from the chimeras, ideas, and dogmas with which I had always identified myself. From Ginsberg I learned to howl and scream at civilization's constricting forms. Freud suggested to me that it was civilization that kept me from the deep dark recesses of myself. I wanted to experience my essence. I wanted to know who I truly was. Bit by bit I struck down the fences.

Polanski and Fellini films could only be truly understood when smoking marijuana. I tried to grasp essence, in and of itself, with a little help from LSD and mescaline. Step by step I descended into emotional and psychological chaos.

I might never have gotten out—a lot of people didn't. A

friend of mine was hospitalized, but we knew that it was society that was sick—we had read *One Flew over the Cuckoo's Nest* and R. D. Laing.

There were a lot of burned-out liberated people who haunted the Rat Cellar, men and women who didn't want to leave it for the ugly, bourgeois, real world. And they never did. They sat there smoking, playing cards, going out (weather permitting) to demonstrate against the Vietnam War, cheering on the younger radicals as they hurled metal garbage cans at the police; as they blew up the Army-Math Research Center; as they set fire to the A&P Supermarket which contained all the awful symbols of an ugly society; as they cursed the National Guard and mocked the Jewish princesses who happened to walk by.

But I was no longer a Jewish princess. Nor was I a radical. I hated politics and socialism and communism and all "isms." I hated the demonstrations and the violence. Yet I was too intensely introverted after all the drugs I had taken to feel comfortable in the happy-go-lucky world of free-loving flower children. I didn't belong anywhere.

In some sense I was ecstatic, full of my individuality, my body, my passions, my power, the potential to be anything pumping through my veins. I was living life dangerously, treading where I should not tread, making myself do what I should not do, breaking down all barriers. I felt like Isadora Duncan, the creative dancer. She became my muse. I called myself Sadora.

I was dreadfully alone. The void left by my mother's dying, the void I had filled with beautiful clothes and plans about glamorous careers and handsome husbands, enveloped me. I scrawled and poured forth in notebooks in a tongue no one could decipher, not even myself. I put on my mother's wedding ring. My umbilical cord to the world had been cut. I didn't want to marry or have children—I married myself to my mother in spirit.

Where can you go when you've destroyed all the roads that lead back? How do you find the way when you've smashed all the landmarks?

July 8

Yossi called me and said, "I learned something from the sea, Ema. From the sea we can learn everything.

"They would take us to the sea on the darkest and stormiest day of winter, when waves, literally walls of fuming water, followed one after the other. We had to dive in. There is no way to fight the waves. You have to let go. You go with the wave by holding your breath, and when it has passed, you breathe again and prepare for the next.

"That's how life is. A wave, then a few seconds to catch your breath for the next wave. I don't get excited or upset when the wave throws me.

"Thrashing and fighting surely brings death."

July 12

There is no way to fight the waves. Hold your breath, breathe again, prepare for the next.

Frank and I came home from Beer Sheba to hear that the murderous insanity has come to the very gates of Kiriat Arba. This morning David Cohen, a contractor working here, was sprayed with bullets as he prepared to leave Kiriat Arba on his way to Hebron.

As we drove into Kiriat Arba, we saw hundreds of our neighbors outside the gate demonstrating in anger and pain.

"Jewish blood cannot be spilled freely!"

We heard shooting coming from every direction. We were told that the Arabs were firing upon the northern Kiriat Arba neighborhood of Harsina. They were firing upon the hilltop across from our house, the one the Israeli army had retaken. They were firing upon the police headquarters across the road in the neighborhood of Givat Avot.

We were told that Miriam had been seen earlier when she returned from three days in Gush Qatif where she worked at a besieged Israeli settlement located on the border with Gaza. She got off the bus in Kiriat Arba and, emotionally overcome, immediately joined the demonstration. But she hadn't been seen since.

She might be outside one of the gates. Frank went there and looked but didn't find her. At eleven o'clock the phone rang. It was a woman telling me that she had seen Miriam being arrested. She was locked up at the police station at Givot Avot which was coming under fire.

In a hail of bullets, Frank and I drove there and arrived unharmed. We were brought to Miriam. She was still being detained.

"Do you know she's only sixteen?" we told the policewomen who were still questioning her.

One of them responded, "We don't know anything about her. She's not cooperating with us. She's not telling us anything. She wouldn't even tell us her name. But minors are not exempt from the law."

"What did she do?" we wanted to know.

Miriam opened her mouth. "They say that in revenge for David's murder I went to an Arab's field and uprooted three of his tomato plants. I didn't do it, but what if I had? What are tomatoes against a life?"

The policewoman said, "She refuses to cooperate. Just been mouthing off like that all night."

"The police deserve it! They protect the Arabs. And us? They've been hitting us!" Miriam cried.

She pushed up the sleeve of her shirt. Indeed, she had bruises.

"We want to file a complaint for police brutality!" Frank exclaimed.

The officer in charge of taking complaints was brought in. Outside, the battle intensified. The Arabs were letting loose with everything they had and we were retaliating in kind. From the conversation between police officers, we understood that Arabs had opened fire on a group of Kiriat Arba settlers who were demonstrating. We heard on the police radios that two people were injured.

We signed Miriam out on bail. At one o'clock in the morning we arrived home.

In the morning the quiet woke me up. It was a quiet that covered something which was not quiet at all. I took our German shepherd out and waited for a neighbor, uncomfortable with it too, to put her head out the window. Gerry appeared above her clotheslines.

"What is it?" I asked.

Softly, as if she were ashamed to say it, she whispered, "Hezzy was killed."

Hezzy Mualam and other members of the Local Council had put on their army uniforms and called a meeting at the junction where Mordecai Lapid and his son, Shalom, had been gunned down in 1993. Baruch Goldstein, our neighbor, had rushed to their aid, and Shalom died in his arms.

So many friends had died in his arms. Many of us think it was that event which broke our neighbor Dr. Goldstein.

Early one Purim morning in February 1994 he put on his army uniform and walked into the Cave of the Patriarchs and Matriarchs, ostensibly to pray.

While the Muslims were prostrate in prayer, he emptied his rifle into them. He killed twenty-nine Arabs before the barrel of his rifle jammed. He tried to make a run for it, but the door leading out of the Cave was bolted. The Arabs who weren't injured smashed Dr. Goldstein with a fire extinguisher until he resembled a bloodied effigy. That's what the soldiers thought his body was.

As Baruch Goldstein had done, the Local Council members put on their army uniforms and went down to Lapid Junction, now a part of the Palestinian Authority. Their intent was to set up a roadblock so that murderers would be unable to get to the Kiriat Arba gates as they had yesterday morning.

In no time Arafat's Force 17 commandos were taxied there in yellow Mercedes sedans. They got the settlers in their cross hairs and pulled their triggers. Everybody dove for cover. Hezzy was hit above his hip bone.

Shmuel ben Bassat was hit a few times in his leg. The army was unable to evacuate either of them because bullets kept flying.

The bullets they used had been outlawed. The bullet that got Hezzy rocketed in spirals through his kidney and lungs. By the time he got to Hadassah Hospital, doctors knew there was nothing they could do. He was a good man who never hurt anyone in his life.

He is survived by four children. Miriam is a friend of his daughter, Raana.

His funeral is this morning. Of course we will all go.

Can it be? That amidst all this pain, prophets are beginning to walk the land? Prophets who do not wear robes or have anything about them that suggests they are extraordinary people?

At an army base in the Negev where Estie went to teach a course on weaponry, she fell ill. The paramedic who treated her was working in the clinic that day to fulfill his army reserve duty. In civilian life he works as an acupuncturist.

Suddenly, as he examined her, his eyes narrowed.

"You have four brothers and sisters." He then proceeded to tell her about each of them.

When he finished describing them, he put his hand to the left side of his face. "Your father," he said, "your father was injured several years ago. Very badly. This side of his face. Intifada?"

Estie swallowed. "Yes. How did you know?"

"Your mother is strong but not strong enough. She feels too insecure in Kiriat Arba. Your mother and father should move out of there.

"It is not a good place for a worrier.

"Estie, when you finish the army leave Israel for awhile. Do like your oldest brother is doing. You've been through too many difficult things."

Estie left the clinic extremely shaken. She told her fellow soldiers how the medic at the clinic was able to read her soul. They went running there to see him.

Oddly enough, they found only a dull medic. Whatever union he had achieved with a cosmic force was no longer operative.

He treated her friends one by one, checked their heartbeats, their pulses, their ears, their tongues. He stuck thermometers in their mouths, so that they couldn't ask him what they should do when they finished the army.

When he took the thermometers out, he offered no advice. He gave one soldier aspirins, to another he gave pills for diarrhea.

They couldn't understand it. The knots of their lives were still tied. No Master had untied them.

July 19

Shmulik wrote, "Too much water has gone under the bridge."

By water, he meant blood. Kiriat Arba will never be the same. The Hebron Hills will not be the same. Estie will never be the same. Shmulik is planning to fly back from New York on September 13 in order to be here for Rosh Hashanah.

He will not come back to the same country. He will find the roads abandoned, newly dug graves and army tanks poised on hilltops. He will find that teenagers he knew are now married and that young girls now cover their heads.

Kiriat Arba–Hebron girls are becoming engaged at sixteen and marrying seventeen- and eighteen-year-old boys.

It is not easy for Miriam to see her peers under the bridal canopy. She and her friends who are not engaged feel undesirable. They are questioning the meaning of their tenth-grade lives. Will they become dried up spinsters as they sit behind their desks in school?

"Why stay in school? The schools belong to the government, and the government doesn't protect us from the Arabs. It is better to find a husband and drop out. The most noble and sacred thing a girl can do is build her own home!"

Yehoshua is having a difficult time too. His best friend is engaged. He and Israel crawled together, toddled together, went to school together, dropped out of school together, built their house at Maon together—the house that was destroyed by the Israeli army. Israel is to marry one of Miriam's friends.

My husband and I are torn between going to these premature weddings and voicing our protest by not going.

In the end, we usually go.

The Hassidic rock band booms on electric guitars and organs, albeit Psalms set to music. The young guests do not dance the traditional Israeli folk dances. The circles of young people holding hands have broken up. They dance alone; the dancing is wild. The smell of marijuana is in the air.

Our peers sit at the tables reserved for the old people, religious Zionist settlers who were once good soldiers and are now too rickety to dance. With canes by their sides and grandchildren on their laps, they watch the revolutionary dancing around the bride and groom. Religious Zionism as we know it is dying.

Our wise men say that a bride and her groom are filled with divine presence. So at each of these weddings, the girls of Kiriat Arba and Hebron stand in line before the bride to receive her blessings; and the boys stand in line before the groom to receive his. The child bride and child groom confer a whispered blessing on each guest—that his or her soul mate will soon appear from heaven.

Our sages say that Rebecca was nine when she married Isaac. Our researchers say that, as in days of old, girls today reach puberty earlier than their mothers did.

So much water has flowed under the bridge. Is it flowing backward?

July 29

It is Tisha B'av, a day of fasting and prayer for religious Jews. On this date thousands of years ago both the First Temple of King Solomon and the Second Temple, built by the returning exiles, were destroyed.

The first was destroyed by the Babylonians in 587 B.C.E. The second was destroyed by the Romans in 70 A.D.

Now Arabs are rioting on the Temple Mount because today, a group called the Temple Mount Faithful is to lay the symbolic cornerstone of the Third Temple in the Old City.

Today there is rioting as thousands of Arabs praying at the Dome of the Rock and other mosques on the Temple Mount, surged out to hurl rocks at the masses of Jews wailing at the Western Wall below, mourning the destruction of their Temple two thousand years ago.

Police wielding plastic body shields rushed the Mount and charged. Some police and many Muslims were injured.

August 9

In spite of all that is happening around us, I have this incredible sense that the sky is opening up. So strong is the sense of the opening of the sky that I have begun a new volume of this diary.

Signaling growth, a flight from old patterns, something being unlocked. Is it a seal?

According to prophetic Kabalists, seals keep our souls confined to our daily existence and blindness. They hold back the cosmic forces that would otherwise flood us. When one is ready, however, a mover will come from the outside to "meet you" at one seal. Just one. He or she may be a medic at a clinic, a neighbor, a physician of the soul.

Who met me? I do not know. I sat down one day in July and prayed. "I know I have blessings," I wept. "But I feel stifled, stopped up in the bottle with them! Please let me breathe a breath of fresh air! Please open a door! Can I go around Jerusalem peddling my tutorial services until I'm an old lady?"

The next day I went to the University for an appointment with a professor about an idea for my master's thesis, "Women in Search of God."

"What do you want to do with your life, June?" he asked at the end of our meeting.

I hedged. "What do you mean? Why are you asking me that? I want to continue teaching my pupils in Jerusalem. Writing my books." Then I blurted out, "You want to know the truth? I'd like to teach at the university level."

"You're on," he said. "How about doing a course on "In Search of Spirituality"?

The pounding of Israeli artillery and tank fire and the popping of Arab rifles has stopped for the time being. For several nights now we can see stars without the paths of tracer bullets. In the morning we have not found dead birds shot out of their trees. We can hear birdsong in the eerie silence of what is perhaps a cease-fire.

The silence covers deep wounds and drastic psychological and spiritual changes in our community, a microcosm, perhaps, of the entire Jewish nation.

August 10

2:15 p.m. Miriam, on a two-day summer vacation, called from Safed to tell me she had just seen a bulletin on television. A suicide bomber just killed himself in the Sbarro Italian fast-food restaurant at the busiest intersection in downtown Jerusalem. It is not yet known how many were killed or injured.

I account for my children and husband.

Frank is in the mountains of Maharastra, India.

Estie is home sleeping after an exhausting few weeks in the army.

Yehoshua is working as a lifeguard.

Shmulik is in California.

I call Yossi, but he doesn't answer. Then he calls me.

Yehoshua calls me.

Everyone is rushing to telephones to find out where their loved ones are.

5:30. The count is now fourteen killed at Sbarro's, including six children. Ninety are injured, three critically. A suicide bomber detonated himself in the restaurant which was packed at lunchtime. The bomb was packed with nails to ensure that injuries would be devastating.

Oh God no.

Among those killed—Tehilla Maoz, who was born and raised in Kiriat Arba until she was six years old. Her brother Naphtali lived with us for a couple of years when their parents were going through a difficult divorce. Tehilla, a beautiful girl, was working at the cash register at Sbarro's, just before she was to begin her National Service.

Killed—five in one family. The Schijveschuurder family, immigrants from Holland: mother, Tzira; father, Mordechai; Hemda, sitting in her stroller; three-year-old Avraham Yitzhak; fourteen-year-old Ra'aya. Two daughters, Chaya, eight, and Leah, ten, were injured. Three sons who didn't join them on their outing were spared.

Spared what? Their twenty-one-year old son had to go to Abu Kabir to identify the five bodies, then to the hospital to visit his badly injured sisters.

In Ramallah, Arabs danced and celebrated in the streets.

The Israeli army and police forces seized PLO and Hamas offices in East Jerusalem, including those in the Orient House.

People here are praying, not for peace but for full-scale war. They are putting stickers on their cars: NO ARABS! NO ATTACKS! MEIR KAHANE WAS RIGHT!

August 14

Miriam went to pay a *shivah* call on the Schijveschuurder family, and I went to visit the family of Tehilla Maoz. Miriam told me the three sons Schijveschuurder are sitting at Bait Neriah in a huge stone house. So cold, Miriam said, so cold. Leah is in the hospital with burns. Chaya was released from the hospital and spoke with reporters. Her words are being reported on television and radio all over Israel.

"Everything that happens here, it's all a miracle. And nothing happens here for no reason. And God knows what he's doing. He wants to tell us that we must behave better. And that soon the Messiah will come. And that then, all dead will rise again."

Is this an eight-year-old girl speaking? Or have cataclysmic events overnight changed this little girl into a wise and ancient soul?

August 15

Shmulik was supposed to fly out of New York on September 13, but all of a sudden felt he wanted to get home sooner. He drove Continental Airlines crazy until they agreed to move his flight to an earlier date.

He is staying in New Jersey now. Every morning he takes

the PATH train to lower Manhattan, gets off at the World Trade Center, sits on the grassy plaza, and absorbs his last few days of pleasure.

He says the energy in New York is incredible. He has never felt anything like it. We keep getting e-mail messages: I LOVE NEW YORK! NEW YORKERS ARE GREAT! He asks if this is because they haven't been beaten down by tragedy upon tragedy, attack upon terrorist attack.

He wishes he were a battery so that he could store up the power and good feelings of New York to help him through the hard days that lie ahead in Israel.

Sitting on the plaza between the north and south Twin Towers, he plans his sight-seeing for each day. He hasn't yet visited the house where I grew up but he doesn't want to return to Israel until he does. He is going to call my childhood friend who still lives on Long Island.

Susie and I used to ask each other, "How many children do you want when you grow up?"

"None," I would reply. "I want to have a career."

If you take out a map of Long Island and look at the North Shore, you'll see the two necklike peninsulas of Nassau County jutting into Long Island Sound. F. Scott Fitzgerald's Gatsby lived on the western peninsula. I lived on the eastern one across the bay, not too far from the Guggenheim estate, Perry Como's mansion, and the palatial home of Mafia boss Frank Costello.

I might still be there now, but something diverted me. Remember the forces in the water beneath the raft?

One was a subconscious recognition that suffering might make us into deeper, more evolved beings.

When my mother was taken from me, I screamed and raged at first that I hated God. But soon I found myself lying on my belly each night, my hands clasped beneath my chin in prayer. For an hour and a half I would thank whoever took and whoever gave.

Within me I felt the throbbing of some sort of wisdom, the hard-won prize after a difficult battle. For three years I prayed. Then I stopped in order to look for new battles, to seek out a new, hard way.

When I first met Frank, he said to me, "Why search for suffering? There is enough in the world; it searches out everybody. It will search for you."

Long after, I stopped pursuing battles and the hard way, when all I wanted was quiet and the pleasure of educating my five children, then suffering found me in Kiriat Arba, Hebron. In its grasp, I raised them.

I believe that the suffering we are all going through will destroy our old selves, will make us more evolved, will crack and crush that in us which is not good enough. I believe that the Messiah is not a person, outside of us, but is a noble state of mind possible in each and every one of us, a state of mind which must be attained, too often through pain.

Just look at Chaya, the eight-year-old girl turned into a prophetess when she was orphaned, and injured, and lost five of her family. Or me, a child, lying on my belly at night, brought to the recognition of an almighty power which takes and gives.

But still sometimes I quiver in fear. And inside I hear a

small voice saying that there must be other and gentler ways to reach a higher state of being. For this I pray—that our path will not be tumultuous and treacherous, that bad things and bad people will not lie in wait along the way.

August 21

This afternoon something brought me to the window. I heard the car door slam. Looking outside I saw a someone strangely familiar. He had a huge backpack on his back and his hair had grown into tight, spirally curls. His blue eyes blazed at me.

"Shmulik!"

I threw open the door and soon my arms were around my first-born son, grown into a man.

We held each other for the longest time.

"So good to be home. So good to be in Kiriat Arba. Israel. You don't know how much I missed you. Nine months is enough. I couldn't stand it anymore."

Our house filled up with so much happiness; we floated on it and filled up with it too.

August 23

Snipers firing from Abu Sneineh shot two brothers in Hebron. The Meshualim boys went up to their roof to hang the laundry for their mother. When they didn't come back down, their mother went up and found them sprawled in blood.

I heard the sirens of the two ambulances that rushed them to the hospital. Tank and rocket fire went on for hours. Then all at once our house shook as in an earthquake. We didn't know why until later.

The army went into Abu Sneineh in the Palestinian Authority to destroy two empty houses that were being continually used to shoot from. They ignited 250 kilograms of explosives. When the job was done, they pulled out.

August 25

Shmulik went up to Samaria to be with Yossi and Adi and to see his baby niece for the first time. Then, he, who is so changed, will begin to put his life together in a country that is also changed.

He will not return to Kiriat Arba to live. He will start at Hebrew University in the fall and live in Jerusalem.

I remember the theme song of Estie's high school graduation and now I cry when I hear its strain:

Little birds leave their nest to fly where they will fly.
But loved birds, do not forget, there are eagles in the sky.

August 26

Fallen prey, a young mother and father on Road 443, the road from Jerusalem to Modiim. The mother lay on her two little children, absorbing the bullets that would have killed them.

Why did these Arabs kill? Why did they fire through the windows of a car carrying, in plain view, two infant daughters and young parents? To create two more orphans? To cut off two more young lives? To cause pain which never ends to the family that survives?

Some years ago, after Dr. Goldstein's massacre in the Cave of the Patriarchs and Matriarchs, David, an old friend of ours, approached us with burning eyes.

"I'm starting a movement of settlers who want peace with the Palestinians. Do you want to join it?"

The movement had one member, him. He was an American and a veteran of the war in Vietnam. As a Marine Corps forward artillery observer, he had probably slain hundreds, if not thousands, of Vietcong.

He told us that after reading about Natzer Yusuf, the head of the Palestinian police, he had had an awakening. Natzer Yusuf had been in Vietnam, too, training in guerrilla warfare with the Vietcong.

"Natzer Yusuf and I could be like brothers! We fought against each other in two wars, Vietnam and Lebanon. But now we're both sick of killing."

Alone, David had gone to the Erez checkpoint, crossed the border with his American passport, and taken a cab to Palestinian police headquarters in Gaza City. There he asked to meet Natzer Yusuf.

The head of Palestinian police welcomed him with a warm hug. He too saw the settlers as potential partners for peace. He invited David to come again with his neighbors.

Thinking we had no choice but to live with the Arabs, since 80 percent of Hebron would be given to them, Frank agreed to take part in David's peace initiative. He was interested mainly in going on behalf of the medical school to establish bioethical and environmental cooperation. Frank believes that no matter what else, we must cooperate on matters of public health—disease-causing bacteria do not acknowledge the fences of partition.

In 1995 my husband traveled with David to Yasir Arafat's provisional headquarters in Gaza several times. Once he took my son, Yossi.

After that he took me. Although we had obtained all the necessary permits from both the Palestinian officials and the Israeli government, we were held up on the Israeli side of the crossing for three and a half hours. Army officers told us they'd never heard of such permits.

After many phone calls we were allowed past the crossing and into an eerie no-man's-strip which separated Gaza, the provisional capital of the Palestinian Authority, from Israel. At the other darkened end, two cars with Palestinian driver/bodyguards awaited us. We got in and were driven at high speed through Gaza, a city we knew well.

When we lived in the Sinai desert, before the peace accords which established the Palestinian Authority, there were no fences and borders between Arabs and Jews. We did all our shopping in Gaza.

We arrived at the Palestinian military headquarters. It looked just as it had when it was the Israeli military headquarters, except that their flag flapped outside and we were the unarmed ones being escorted up the stairs by armed Arabs. We were taken to the office of the high commander, Major General Natzer Yusuf. A Major Farid and his young underling and driver, Mohammed, stood by.

They hugged and kissed David on both cheeks and he kissed their cheeks, the first Israeli settler to do so. They shook Frank's hand and mine. Then we were led to a room with full-length curtains and sofas where Arab servants brought us tea and coffee with cloves.

General Natzer Yusuf made a few opening remarks. ("You can see the Marxist dialectic at work.") And then we were divided into two groups. Frank and his colleagues from the medical school went to meet with Arab health officials about a bioethics program for Palestinian doctors and nurses. David went into closed chambers to talk with Natzer Yusuf, Major Farid, and

Mohammed about security arrangements for Jews who might choose to live under the Palestinian Authority rather than move from Kiriat Arba, Hebron.

I felt a small thrill. I was out of the ghetto. A ghetto defined as much by the barbed ideology within it as by the wire fence around it. An ideology that excluded everything and everyone unlike itself. I decided to continue to take part in this grassroots peace initiative; I was taking myself beyond Kiriat Arba and into a future I would have a hand in making.

Before this meeting on October 4, 1995, we had been feeling like helpless souls in the hands of a faceless and ruthless ruling clique. Kiriat Arba, Hebron, was the trump card of this elite. This feeling of helplessness, which persisted for many years, caused me much distress and a marked deterioration in health. I was beginning to look and feel like an old lady.

But how could I go so easily from being a settler to being a "collaborator," as one good friend called me? Because I never saw myself as a settler. We were different. We were "the other," with too wide a worldview.

My husband answered right-wing friends, "We never drove the Arabs out. And they're not leaving of their own accord. They're here to stay and so are we. We have a reality no one foresaw. A Palestinian Authority with Jewish settlements."

David was meeting with the Palestinian High Command trying to get an agreement whereby Jews who wanted to could buy land, houses, or apartments in the autonomous areas. The Palestinians made a gracious offer of Palestinian citizenship to the settlers.

All this depended, of course, on whether or not Natzer

Yusuf took control of Hebron. The commander of Hebron might also be Colonel Jibril Rajoub, a hard-line Hamas fundamentalist responsible for the torture and death of many Arabs in Hebron. Rajoub had vowed to kill Jews as well.

An hour later, as we were driven back at breakneck speed to no-man's-land, David told us about his meeting. "I asked them what their agenda was."

Then he laughed weakly. "They told me the most valuable thing they learned from the Vietcong.

"'Never state what your aims are. Never let the enemy know what you want. Don't tell them why you kill.'"

Frank, David, and others continued to meet with Natzer Yusuf and Major Farid in Gaza. One day David asked Natzer, "When will you stop killing my friends?"

He was referring to fellow settlers who were being murdered in drive-by shootings throughout Judea and Samaria.

Natzer Yusuf replied, "I can't promise that no one will attack you. But I do promise you that I will take revenge against anyone who does. And I will make that known."

From the time Natzer Yusuf made his promise to David, there were no more attacks in Judea and Samaria. All the terror attacks took place within the pre-1967 borders.

But in September 1996 David informed us that Major Farid had been hauled away by Arafat's secret police and had, for some time now, been hanging by his feet in his jail cell in Ramallah. This was confirmed by Amnesty International.

After being cut down from the ropes that tied him, Major Farid was thrown from a second-story window during further interrogation. He was brought to Shefa Hospital in Gaza, suffering from multiple fractures and internal injuries. This was confirmed by a pro-Arab American activist living in Hebron.

Mohammad, Major Farid's underling, died during torture.

Natzer Yusuf was last seen by David in Jerusalem on his way, presumably, to seek refuge in Jordan.

David contends that the American CIA backed the terrorist Rajoub. He knows that CIA agents met with Rajoub in Taba to make the Hamas covenant more amenable to Israel. When that was done, they cooperated in his takeover of Hebron.

Do not ask why. Just know that the chambers of those who rule the world are dark and sinister and too convoluted for the likes of Frank and me.

So we cursed them silently. And in silence we buried our short-lived dream.

August 27

Two more have fallen, though I heard there may be more.

Dov Roizman, aged fifty-eight, was shot to death last night when he went into Area B, to an Arab village under the military control of the Israeli Defense Forces.

Another friend of my boys has been murdered on a road near Yossi's home at Ittamar.

Meir Lixemberg, age thirty-eight, father of five, was shot in the head. My sons visited him at his home on Friday. His children ran about and his wife prepared for the Sabbath. Meir had just caught a mouse. Still in its trap, the mouse was frantically trying to get out.

"Why don't you drown it?" Shmulik suggested.

"Then it would suffer." Meir said. "I'll let it go."

My sons walked outside with him. At a distance from his house, he squatted down and opened the trap door.

"But it's going to come back," Shmulik said.

"Sure," Meir said. "They always do."

Three days later Meir was killed while sitting in the back seat of a car traveling on the pastoral road that runs from Ittamar to the settlement of Har Baracha, the Mount of Blessings.

Is this a Zen Buddhist koan? A riddle which demands to be answered but cannot be? How can a man who couldn't kill a mouse have his brains blown out near the Mount of Blessings?

August 31

Gun battles for several nights and we cannot sleep. Fatigued, we get out of bed and go to the lawn overlooking the old city of Hebron. We watch as a circle of fire bursts out of an abandoned house at Abu Sneineh that the Israeli tanks have hit. The Arab gunmen continue their attack.

Our ears have become more finely attuned. The Arabs are now using anti-tank grenades and mortar rounds. This, they say, is in retaliation for Israel's targeted missile attacks against several

Palestinian military and police buildings elsewhere in the West Bank.

In the cross fire an eleven-year-old boy in the Jewish neighborhood of Hebron was lightly wounded by shrapnel.

David, our "peacenik" friend, joins us on the lawn. He says that the people here are experiencing combat fatigue just like the American soldiers in Vietnam.

Perhaps that explains the odd behavior we have witnessed lately.

Jewish youths have been going up to the rooftops of the apartment buildings here, throwing off the army's sandbags, then heaving the bulletproof posts five stories down to the ground below.

As another circle of fire burst out of the wall of the house below, David remarked. "Looks impressive, but it's not. The Israeli Defense Force (IDF) keeps hitting the same empty building. No one's lived there in months. They've got to go into Abu Sneineh and take the whole neighborhood, but they won't because they know we won't win the next war. The Arab countries have been supplied with arsenals of anthrax, and Israel has no defense.

"We've got no choice but to play along with the American-sponsored peace."

"What about God's fighting for the Jewish people?" I ask. "We were always outnumbered against terrible enemies, yet when God was with us, we won."

"When God tells us what to do, we'll do it," David replies. "Right now he ain't talking. So we'll continue as we are, building an Arab-Israeli confederation under the Americans. This confederation will take over all the water and oil resources of the Middle East."

The young boy injured by shrapnel was Miriam Ze'ev's son. Miriam is an American immigrant. Two months ago her daughter Iska's cheek was grazed by a bullet.

We used to exist on miracles, now we exist on misses. Either the bullets have not hit, or they have missed crucial organs. So many varieties of misses each day, we hardly take notice.

I think I ought to tell you this one before it slips from my memory.

Estie's gradeschool teacher and her family were in their apartment at Bait Hadassah dressing for her son's wedding when bullets started whizzing above their heads. Someone grabbed a rifle and began shooting back toward Abu Sneineh. Israeli soldiers rushed up the stairs, and a scuffle broke out as the soldiers tried to disarm the person shooting. An officer in the army injured the groom. As he began to bleed profusely, Arabs shot again. This time two soldiers were hit and lightly wounded.

And the once-happy mother of the groom? A bullet tore through the shoulder of her bathrobe. She had to offer the *gomel*, the prayer made for escaping death or injury.

September 3

In spite of all the tragedies and near tragedies around me, for me personally, the sky continued to open up.

I was offered a position lecturing on "Spiritual Literature" for one semester at Ben Gurion University. Photographs of mine, along with an article about my husband's health-education team in India, had run in the Israeli *National Geographic*. An article of mine about Untouchable women was to appear in Ralph Nader's magazine, *Essential Information*.

I feel guilty with my happiness about my personal blessings. After all, three bombs went off in Jerusalem yesterday. Three people were slightly wounded.

On the road Frank drives every day to and from Beer Sheba, the former mayor of the Hebron Hills was injured by shrapnel.

For the past hour and a half we have been listening to Israeli tanks and machine guns firing at the Palestinian military headquarters in Hebron. It sits atop a mountain ridge named after a famous sheikh, Harat al-Sheikh. Much of Arab Hebron lies on and below that ridge, and from there Arab gunmen shoot at the Jewish neighborhood of Tel Romeida.

Hearing sirens, I went outside and saw two of our ambulances speeding down to Hebron. At least one Israeli soldier had been hit and maybe a civilian too. As I watched from a point where I had a panoramic view of Hebron, our neighbor Arieh came up to me. For years he had traveled around the world, finally settling down in Israel. In 1969 he was among the first religious Zionists who insisted on resettling Hebron after the Six-Day War. At the time they were allowed to live only at the Israeli military headquarters.

Some time later he moved to Kiriat Arba. For years he has supported his family by buying cleaning fluids from the Arabs and reselling them. The Oslo peace accords did not deter him—though Jews were no longer allowed to enter the Arab sectors of Hebron, he was able to get through freely and without a weapon.

Last year he had just settled into the cracked and faded chair of his favorite Arab barber when the Palestinian police walked in. Before the scissors touched his hair, he was escorted out of Arab-controlled Hebron and told to have his hair cut somewhere else.

"Why don't we just go in and take Abu Sneineh?" I asked him.

In his Brooklyn-Queens twang he said, "See? That would leave Harat al-Sheikh where most of the Arab population lives and where the Palestinian Authority rules from."

He pointed to the military headquarters where he used to live. During the pullback it had been handed over to the Palestinian Authority.

"The army would have to conquer *that.* In other words, get it? *All* Hebron."

The word travels up to us. The two injured in Hebron were Israeli soldiers. An explosive charge was thrown at them at Aaron Gross Square in the Jewish sector of Hebron. The square is named after our friend Aaron, the son of American immigrants, who was knifed to death in Hebron in 1982. Frank shot at Aaron's attackers but was too far away to kill them.

According to one account, Frank succeeded in wounding one of them, and this helped the police apprehend the murderers. But Frank is not certain. What is certain is that the killers were sentenced to life imprisonment and were later released in the "Jabril Deal" of prisoner exchange.

In retaliation for the explosive charge that was thrown earlier today, and for the shooting of the former mayor of the Hebron Hills, Israeli forces fired rockets into the Palestinian military headquarters on Harat al-Sheikh.

September 10

Yossi, Adi, and their daughter Shachar have moved to the Hebron Hills, to an outpost with one other family eleven miles south of here. The outpost is named for Yair Har Sinai, who was killed near there as he pastured his sheep.

Yossi missed the Hebron area terribly. He wants to be near the land where he spent his childhood. He wants to be near us. It is a time for family members to seek comfort and warmth from one another in order to gather strength.

Today a suicide bomber blew himself up at the Nahariya Railway Station in the north of Israel. Today terrorists shot and killed a teacher and her driver on their way to school in the Jordan Valley.

Today Yossi calls at 1:30 p.m. to ask where Estie is. I tell him she's on her way to her army base at Bait Lid. I ask why he wants to know.

"There was just a terrorist attack at Bait Lid Junction where Estie gets off her bus."

I exhale slowly and try to stay calm. I call her mobile phone. It is turned off.

I sit down with my pendulum and ask permission to use it. I first learned how to use a pendulum from Irena, a bioenergy healer who immigrated from Russia to Kiriat Arba. She taught me how to hold a double thread with a needle dangling from it to find out which foods were suitable for me and which were not. The unconscious mind, which is very knowing, causes the needle to move in either a positive or negative direction.

Excited by the gift Irena brought from behind the Iron Curtain, I showed my children. Immediately they prepared their own pendulums. For a long time my children would ask, "Am I allergic to white flour? Will sugar make me hyperactive?"

A few years later Irena showed me how to use the pendulum for more serious questions. Russian immigrants came to Irena all the time to find out if the relatives they hadn't heard from were alive or dead, and if alive, where they might be found.

Now I asked the pendulum, "Is Estie alive and well?"

"Yes."

"Is she at her army base?"

"Yes."

Ten minutes later she called. Moments of relief, then sickness with it all.

Judaism was suppressed in my childhood home because it was associated with too much suffering. The establishment of a Jewish state was to be the panacea for the tortured Jew. Yet statehood has been no cure.

I put my pendulum back in its box.

It is palpably dark, this thick, heavy cynicism, oozing from me. Gaps of meaning, they call it. I have fallen into one.

My daughter has fallen into something too. Jolted out of a nap she was taking on Shabbat, Miriam came into the living room with glazed and frightened eyes. "I have to pray. I have to pray. If I don't something bad is going to happen." She grabbed a Book of Psalms, then rocking back and forth, she furiously moved her lips.

"Do you feel better?" I asked.

"No!" she cried. "I can't explain it."

September 11

A plane came out of the sky and crashed into one of the Twin Towers of the World Trade Center in Manhattan, ripping into its uppermost stories, causing explosions and fires. Word spread through Israel. Yehoshua and I ran to the home of my neighbor, Aliza, to watch it on television. And as we watched fire billow out of the upper floors, a second plane flying horribly low flew into the other tower, leaving an inferno.

I look at my son. He looks at me. Are we experiencing reality together, or are we together in a dream? Our hands cover our mouths and we do not talk. In silence we watch one of the towers collapse in a cloud of cinders and debris onto the sidewalks of New York City.

They say fifty thousand people work in the Twin Towers. Another ninety thousand pass through there each day. Two hundred firemen who were helping evacuate the first building are missing and presumed dead. Newscasters say the planes were hijacked.

Then, a half-hour later, another hijacked plane crashes into the Pentagon, in the capital, the center of the American military and defense system. Hundreds of people, including the passengers on the plane, are presumed killed.

Soon after, fixed in our chairs, we witness the collapse of the second Twin Tower.

A fourth plane was apparently hijacked. It was headed toward Washington, D.C. Soon we heard that it had crashed over a shopping center in Pittsburgh.

"Mom." Yehoshua said. And that's all he could say.

Aliza and her husband just shake their heads. This couldn't happen in America. America was safe.

America was a symbol of everything Israel didn't have. Boundaries that enclosed vast territory with waterfalls that in five minutes could provide Israel with all the water it needs for a year. Knowing that when you left home, you would come back alive and whole. Comfortable that no enemies lived among you.

A life human beings should live. Safe, secure, and sound—just like the dollar. Nothing like the shekel. Nothing like it at all.

September 12

I should be preparing for my university teaching which begins next week, but I can't. The atmosphere is so strange. Astronauts orbiting above earth reported to NASA that they noticed quaking along the entire eastern seaboard of the United States.

The shaking is getting here too. I just had to go outside. I got on my bicycle and pedaled to my grocery store followed by our dog. There I can ground myself because the High Holy Days are coming up and there is much to buy. Usually at this time there is a holiday frenzy in the air. But not today.

There is something terribly wrong with the sky today. It is too bright for autumn, yet washed out at the same time—yellow with streaks of darkness. It is too quiet, just as it was after our friend Hezzy was shot, as it was after our Dr. Goldstein shot and killed twenty-nine Arabs. As if the heavens had accomplished some purpose and could now rest. I thought I understood the purpose—that the sky was opening for me, for me. How selfish I was!

Perhaps I did have premonitions about the skies opening and great changes taking place. But I am no prophetess. I did not foresee that the skies would open to this.

Outside the grocery, under the large awning, neighbors

gathered around the newspaper stands, leafing through the papers to see pictures of the hijacked planes crashing into the World Trade Center and the Pentagon. Now and again they stepped over to the fruit and vegetable stands to remind themselves that Rosh Hashanah was coming. Apples and pomegranates were on display. A neighbor held a half-filled bag of carrots. (In Hebrew the word for "carrot" and "decree" are the same. We put carrots on the table, make a blessing over them, then taste them as we hope to taste good decrees in the new year. Not like what happened to America.)

"Those poor people," she mutters. "A lot of Jews were killed too. There was a young woman from Ashkelon on one of the planes."

My widowed friend with a fish head in her hands said, "Didn't Rabbi Meir Kahane predict that America would be the land of the next Holocaust? Jews are going to have to wake up and make *aliya* to Israel. Mark his words, there'll be a mass immigration from America now. And it will be good for us. Good for Israel."

I was about to fill up a bag with apples. But my neighbor said, "Wait. Do you think it was the Japanese who did it? I read that it was Japanese radicals avenging the atom bombs the U.S. dropped on them."

"I hope not." Someone pressed his fingernail into an avocado. "Too ripe," he said, and then, "It would be best for us if it were Arabs."

"Of course it was Arabs," my widowed friend answered. "*Baruch Hashem*. Thank God. Now the Americans can understand how we feel."

A little neighbor with a New York accent paused with a fresh loaf of bread tucked under his arm. "Maybe now the Americans will stop tying our hands and let us strike back at *our* Muslims."

"Clinton never let us chase them after they attacked. He wouldn't let us go into their villages before the attacks when we knew what they were planning and where their weapons were being stored."

"You think Bush will give Ariel Sharon a freer hand now?"

"*He* will. But our leftists won't. The Israeli army could now go into Abu Sneineh and America wouldn't stop them. But in a second Peace Now would be in Hebron demonstrating with the Arabs."

Frank arrived at the grocery store too. On his way to Beer Sheba, he parked his red Citroen by the curb. Someone said to him, "Can you believe what terrorism has come to?"

Frank was very critical. "If you take the number of people killed in the attacks on America against the total population, and compare that with the number of people we have lost to terrorism from our tiny population, you'll find that we have had much worse terrorism. So what do you mean, 'what terrorism has come to'?

"All of a sudden terrorism just arrived in the world? And what about the day-to-day terrorism in Sri Lanka? In the Kashmir?

"Is English-speaking blood better?"

As always, Frank's reaction is unsympathetic with America. He is from Cleveland. I always told him if he had come from a nice place in America like New York, he wouldn't be such a fanatical Zionist.

He kissed me goodbye. I begged him to be careful.

"Don't forget to buy lots of sweet wine for Rosh Hashanah," he said.

September 13

Israel is on high alert now. We all remembered when America attacked Iraq during the Gulf War and Iraq fired missiles at Israel. We had to run into our sealed-off houses and put suffocating gas masks on ourselves and on our children.

The American government is saying that a Saudi Arabian exile, Osama bin Laden, and his terrorist network, Al Qaeda, planned and carried out the attacks. Bin Laden, a multimillionaire, finances, recruits, and trains Sunni Islamic extremists to make a *jihad* against Jews and Crusaders.

President Bush declared the attacks an act of war and said America would go to war in return.

The vibrations that stir America are reaching here. Ariel Sharon proclaimed a national day of mourning yesterday.

Many things bind us to America now. Bin Laden's hatred of Israel and America binds us.

There are many immigrants from America, and they still have relatives there. Most Israelis have some family member who left Israel and made *yerida,* that is, descended to live in America. A woman named Tzippy told me her brother's son works in the World Trade Center but for some reason didn't get to work on time that day.

An estimated four thousand Israelis were in the area of the Twin Towers when they were attacked. Frank's colleague was sitting in an office just across the street from the Twin Towers writing e-mails to his friends and family when it all happened before his eyes. He continued to write, describing everything he saw.

Because we live in one world, whoever thinks that this is a tragedy just for the Americans is wrong. Our destinies are intertwined. Global karma, I believe they call it.

While I was trying to prepare for my classes at the university and finding it difficult to concentrate, Aliza from upstairs excitedly knocked on my door. Behind her stood an official-looking man holding a clipboard.

She was still wearing her apron which was spotted with flour and cocoa. It was Thursday, the day on which religious housewives begin their preparations for the Sabbath. Two days after that would be Rosh Hashanah. There was enough to do and think about without this. "He wants to see if the bomb shelter is in order."

Some years ago Yehoshua, and Aliza's son, Israel, who were best friends before Israel's marriage, made the bomb shelter into their clubhouse. They cleared away years of accumulated castoffs, crates, boxes, broken bicycles, old clothing, and dead cats. They set up a Ping-Pong table, a sofa, and two swivel chairs.

The official introduced himself to me with a Russian accent. He was the inspector for the Local Council. We led him into the shelter.

"Very nice," he remarked. "But the water tank is no good. It's made of asbestos and no longer certified. You will have to buy a new water tank."

"Buy a new water tank?" Aliza asked almost in tears. "When I go around this building asking the tenants to give four shekels a month for the electricity for the hallway lights, they complain. How am I going to make them chip in for a water tank?"

"Tell them America is going to war, and *they* are going to be bombed."

September 14

While I was still outside pinning up our sheets on the clothesline, the phone rang. I hurried inside. Estie was calling from the army. "Have you heard from Rob?" She has called several times asking about my brother and other relatives.

I told her again. "I've tried calling many times. All the lines are still busy."

When she went to America last year to visit, Rob sent a chauffeured limousine to pick her up and drive her to his weekend home in the Hamptons. Shmulik, when he was in New

York, spent an evening with him too. Rob took him out to eat. On Shmulik's first visit to a nonkosher restaurant, he ordered lobster tail, then went to the men's room to vomit.

Aside from these rare visits of my children, we rarely correspond with one another.

"Don't you care?" Estie asked.

"Yes, I do. Of course I do." I was feeling so many things rushing up in crosscurrents that I couldn't speak.

"Ema, are you still on the line?

"Did you ever go to the World Trade Center?"

"You won't believe this," I said. "Though I could see the towers from my windows, I was never inside."

"What windows?"

"Look, Estie, my wash is molding in the bucket outside. You're coming home for Rosh Hashanah. I'll tell you then."

"What are you going to cook for the holidays?"

"How does chicken sound?"

"No, make something good. Make lasagne!"

"For the Jewish New Year you want Italian food?"

September 18

The blast of the ram's horn is coming from one synagogue and now another, heralding the awesome fact: it is the first day of Rosh Hashanah. A new year is being ushered in.

The book of our lives has been opened once again and the Almighty will inscribe decrees for us for the coming year.

Frank, Shmulik, and I stop to listen. Then we begin our walk down to Hebron. Estie did not want to come with us. She never wants to see Hebron again.

We wish the Israeli soldiers at their post, "*Shana Tova*."

"Watch yourselves," they say.

After the murder of Yeshiva student Erez Shmuel, the passages that lead from the alley into the labyrinths of the *casbah,* the Arab market, were sealed off with cement blocks in order to make attacks more difficult.

Still, we spin around to look behind us. There's a manhole where Arabs hammered through the blocks. There are the rooftops of the mildewed and moss-grown buildings which shadow the arches and alleys of the *casbah*, a terrorists' den.

Frank has his hand on his pistol; Shmulik has his hand on his.

But we feel better now. The moldering alley has opened up, and in place of the darkness there is light.

We are at the Cave of the Patriarchs and Matriarchs. Inside, Yehoshua and Miriam are praying.

Somewhere below our feet, in a large cave which extends into many smaller chambers, all our foremothers and fathers are buried. All except for Rachel.

Above their sacred tombs is the monumental structure built almost 2,200 years ago to house a synagogue for their descendants.

The once-peaceful plaza before the Cave has been turned

117

into a military garrison. An Israeli police barracks has been set up. At the Jewish entrance to the Cave, the police set up a depository for weapons; all settlers must hand over their guns, nail clippers, can openers, and scissors before going through the electronic metal detectors.

Behind the electronic gates are more soldiers—border police and "blue" police who monitor the alarm that is frequently set off by the gold fillings in the teeth of old ladies. Frightening as it is to them, they suffer near heart attacks when they find themselves at gunpoint being asked to hand over their bags.

Tourists from all over the world used to come to visit. But this year tourists have taken Israel off their lists of vacation spots. The Arab souvenir shops are shut. Their shops used to be full of famous Hebron glass.

Gone are the Arabs in their *kefiyot* headdresses, smoking on straw stools before the shops with the skirts of their tunics rolled up to their knees, and old chins propped on old canes.

The stalls and shops with their metal doors once flung open to display huge sacks of lima beans and grains were closed. On many of the locked doors Stars of David were painted: SHAL-HEVET'S BLOOD CRIES OUT!

REVENGE! DEATH TO THE ARABS!

The dimly lit coffee shops were closed. There ancient Arabs who witnessed the 1929 pogroms against the Jewish community of Hebron once sat ruminating, running their beads through their fingers over cups of coffee spiced with cloves.

Right after the signing of the peace accords, when it was decided that Israel would relinquish control over many cities in

Judea and Samaria, journalists, reporters, and cameramen from all over the world would sit and drink here too. Often they would get up to film Israeli soldiers, kids who looked so militant in their bulletproof vests, their rifles slung over their shoulders.

But lately there are few Arab children pestering the soldiers for their rations of chocolate milk and running away with smiles. Few Arabs schoolgirls walk by the way they used to, in uniform dresses worn over pants, their hair covered with scarves fastened under their chins.

No Arab women in long black dresses come in from the villages, trekking out with gas balloons and sacks of potatoes on their heads.

In days of old we would have seen the bearded face of a religious Muslim and known he was a member of Hamas. His eyes would be full of hatred. Frank and my sons would not have greeted him, but they would have greeted each and every clean-shaven Arab.

"Id Sayid!" Happy Holiday! And they would greet us in return.

The peace process changed this city; Hebron was divided like Berlin.

This year's terror contributed to the drastic changes too.

When there are too many incidents the army closes off the Arab areas from the Israeli-controlled sector. Too many Arabs have become Hamas. They fire their weapons, throw hand grenades, wire themselves with bombs. But if a period of time goes by without an attack, the army opens the Israeli-controlled streets to Arab life once again.

It wasn't only that the shops and stalls were closed. We had seen that before. But when we looked past our streets into the Arab-controlled sector, we saw little sign of life there either.

Rumor has it that twenty thousand Arabs have fled the city. As in Lebanon, when the PLO took over hospitals, schools, and homes for use in their operations, the Hebron Arabs have found their homes used by terrorists to shoot into the Jewish neighborhoods. When the IDF retaliated, many of them found themselves in the cross fire.

"What do you want?" an Arab working in Kiriat Arba complained to my husband. "Arafat didn't come by himself. You brought him here. He milks us dry, then Hamas comes around and we have to pay them the rest of our money so that we can be protected against the other terrorist groups."

Another Arab cried to my friend, "You Jews are supposed to be smart. Everybody thinks you are, at least. But you're not smart.

"When we lived here under Jordanian rule, all the land belonged to King Hussein and we sweated." He pointed to his forehead. "To till, and plant, and harvest, and we paid *him* taxes.

"When you Jews came we were afraid of you because you were strong. We would have been your serfs too, but what did you do? You said this land was *ours!*

"That's smart? Why couldn't you understand the Arab mentality? We admire fierceness and strength! We see goodwill as weakness. After you conquered here in 1967, you changed our donkeys into Mercedes Benzes! You changed us from being serfs into *enfeddi*, big people, important people!

"Why were you so weak with us? Where is your strength

and pride? Can't your leaders understand that by giving Arabs power here you've made our lives miserable?"

Since September 11, Israeli troops have surrounded the Arab city of Jenin—a prelude, it is believed, to penetration into the city itself. Many of the suicide bombers have come from Jenin. The Israeli Defense Forces may go in and wipe out their training centers.

A few days ago, after a long siege, the IDF moved into Jericho for the first time since it was handed over to Arafat. IDF bulldozers razed the training center for the Palestinian Authority's forces. Then the IDF entered Ramallah with tanks and jeeps, retaliating against two more murders of Israelis.

Yesterday Arafat called for a cease-fire. He is afraid of the green light.

Usually Arabs like the color green. They paint parts of their houses with it to ward off evil spirits. But this green would be different. It would be a green light from America. Go ahead. Go back into all those areas you gave to the Palestinian Authority. Wipe out the infrastructure of the Palestinian Authority. They cannot be partners in peace.

The settlers would interpret this green light differently. Go ahead. Go back into all those areas you gave to the Palestinian Authority. Whack them and smack them the way you did in biblical times. The Redemption is at hand.

One green light could change the face of this city forever.

My Russian bioenergy healer says that Kiriat Arba and Hebron are filled with souls. Souls who died here while fighting with the

Maccabees. Souls who were sacrificed to the Goddess of Hebron when the Romans ruled here. She sees souls here from the Spanish expulsion. Souls who were killed by the Turks.

Irena can see all this on the faces here. Souls that perished during the Mamelukes, when the petty sheikhs ruled; souls who refused to leave Hebron when exiled by the Crusaders; souls who were in Hebron in 1929 when the Arabs killed sixty-three Jewish neighbors and friends. She says that all these deep and mighty souls must be here now for the battle that lies before us.

Arriving outside the ancient Abraham Avinu Synagogue just in time to hear the final blowing of the *shofar*, we cannot help but stand stark still. The daughter of Yonah is playing there. Our friend Yonah was stabbed during the more primitive period of Arab terrorism. He recuperated from the attack but soon after developed brain cancer. His daughter was conceived when he was dying. She was born after his death.

Inside, the men draped in their white prayer shawls are swaying and reciting the blessings which must be made before the blowing of the *shofar*.

Behind the partition, in the back of the synagogue, the women now stand. They push back the crimson cushions of their seats and part the lace curtain that hangs over the grille in order to peek through.

We see Chaya in profile. She wears white and holds a prayer book to her heart. A towering figure, and not only in height. An immigrant from Holland and a convert to Judaism, she had finally found the man she wanted to settle down with, Raphael, a convert from Holland too. Her two children from a previous marriage loved him very much. They had a happy and harmonious family. Raphael was in bliss, he told my husband.

Four months after they were married, he was shot to death on the road to Hebron, together with their good friend Margolit.

Standing beside Chaya is Rivka, the grandmother of the baby Shalhevet who was slain as her mother pushed her down the street in her stroller. Rivka is the wife of Avraham who, on his way to the Cave years before, was jumped by three Arabs who crushed his skull and mouth with an ax. She is the mother of twin girls: Oriah whose baby Shalhevet was shot to death; and Orital, who was stabbed in front of the hundreds of police brought in to maintain order the day the Arabs held their elections in Hebron.

The *shofar* is mute again, and a few minutes later the services are over. The souls are flowing out of the synagogue— women from the women's section, men from the men's. They are saying, "It should only be a good year. God willing. God willing."

"Ah, Shmulik! World traveler, welcome back. *Shana Tova!*" Several men greet him.

"You were in America? You were in New York?"

"The last week of my trip. I was at the World Trade Center every day," Shmulik replied. "I would have been there on September 11 too, except I just had a feeling that I had to get out of there and back to Israel."

"Did you bless God?"

"In my heart I did."

"God did a miracle for you."

"I think so."

"*Nu?* What's going to be? Who are the Americans declaring war on? Osama bin Laden?"

"We can't fathom them. They're going to bring battleships halfway around the world to go against one terrorist hiding deep down in a mountain cave?"

"And they haven't been allowing us into Arab villages and cities to chase after a whole nest of them? Bunch of hypocrites."

"We're outside four Arab villages now!" Shmulik reminds him.

Someone answers, "We need a green light? We need Bush? Bush's ancestors were still swinging in the trees when we gave the world the Torah."

"*Am Yisrael*, the children of Israel, have lost all sense of who they are! We have to ask Bush for a green light? Whoever heard of such a thing."

"We have the green light from '*Ha Kodesh Baruch Hu*'—God."

"From your lips to his ears," his wife says.

"Speedily," a neighbor adds.

"In our days."

September 19

It is the second day of Rosh Hashanah. The cease-fire is holding and our soldiers have been thinned out in this area. We feel their absence at the gate of Kiriat Arba and upon the hilltop across the way in the fortified Arab school. I do not see our flag. Nor do I see our soldiers on the rooftops of the Arab apartments just up the block and across the valley.

Sharon has promised to pull the IDF out of all Arab areas entered this week. He has also promised that there will be no further offensives as long as the quiet holds.

For some reason we have been arguing a lot this holiday. Shmulik is in a terrible mood. Sometimes I wish he were back in America or in Ecuador writing us his beautiful letters.

September 20

Sarit Amrani was killed. Sarit and her husband grew up here. They were in Kiriat Arba with their little children to visit her parents during the two days of Rosh Hashanah. But her mother begged them not to leave for their own home near Bethlehem last night when the holiday was over. She wanted them to travel in the morning when daylight would make the trip safer.

At 7:30 in the morning, not far from their home in Gush Etzion, at a junction where Yehoshua stands so often to hitch a ride to the farm where he works, Arabs in a truck fired down into Sarit's car. Sarit was killed instantly. Her husband was critically injured. Her three children, including a three-month-old infant, were left crying in their seats.

Sarah Nakshon got a phone call. Everyone knows to call

Sarah when there is dire need. One of the first settlers to come to Hebron, she is known as a *tzadayket,* a holy woman.

"Sarah, can you find a wet nurse for Sarit Amrani's baby?"

Sarah searched the Kiriat until she found a new mother whose breasts were full of milk. The orphaned infant was brought to her and the woman cuddled her and cried over her as the infant suckled at her breast.

September 23

Every time America or the European Union puts pressure on Israel to open up the roadblocks around Arab villages because the poor Palestinians are suffering, the result is imprinted in our flesh.

Every time Arafat calls for a cease-fire and we pull back our army, the result is imprinted in our flesh.

Sarit is dead. Her husband is lying in the hospital terribly injured. Her infant will be weaned into the reality of the Middle East.

President George Bush is pressuring Israel to proceed with the meeting with Arafat, in effect legitimizing Arafat's policy of condemning terrorism while secretly endorsing it.

We peep at one another like figurines on the mantle in Agatha Christie's book *And Then There Were None.* So who will be killed next?

When Ariel Sharon canceled the slated meeting between

Shimon Peres and Arafat because of Sarit's murder, I hugged Miriam when she came home from school. We put on music and felt happy.

But Foreign Minister Peres says that to cancel the meeting makes it appear that we're vetoing the American peace initiative.

September 25

Miriam and I did not enjoy calmness of soul for very long.

President Bush is putting together a coalition of countries to fight the terrorists in Afghanistan.

Shimon Peres is dying to be in this coalition. Because the American president wants Arafat to be in the coalition too, Peres wanted to demonstrate that he can work with him.

So he went ahead and met with Arafat at an airport in Gaza, despite the fact that our General Security Services insists that Arafat is behind all the terrorism in Israel, formerly as chairman of the PLO and lately as chairman of the Palestinian Authority.

He is their Most Wanted Man, dead or alive.

September 27

We are fasting today, and Miriam is wearing white. Neither Miriam nor Yehoshua are wearing leather. They are praying all day at the Cave, and the ram's horn is blown once again.

Today is Yom Kippur. The last day of the ten days of repentance, it is the Day of Awe. The gates of heaven are still open for last-minute repentance, but time is running out. At nightfall the gates will slam shut.

I received a letter from Robert yesterday. On it was a long string of names—lawyers in the law firm in which he is junior partner. I tore open the letter. His handwriting was almost illegible. He was in so much pain, it came through in every barely formed letter. He had watched the attack and the collapse of the World Trade Center from the patio of his sixteenth-floor Park Avenue office. Many of his close friends were inside the collapsed towers.

He said he understood me better now.

When did we stop understanding each other? When I left him and went to college?

Was it when I took an apartment off the Bowery, where bums sprawled on the pavement below?

"Why are you living here? Why?" Rob wanted to know when he came to visit me just that one time. He was in my apartment only ten minutes when a fire broke out below and we had to escape to the street.

"I want to experience life," I tried to explain.

"You're speaking strangely."

"Look, you want to *become* something," I said.

"You bet."

"I just want to *be*."

He raised his head and gazed up at the newly completed Twin Towers. "I want to be a big lawyer," he said.

I don't want to get to heaven that way, I thought.

The fire was extinguished. We went back up to my apartment.

In the morning I was to drive him to his summer job in New Hampshire. But when we came down to the street my car was sitting on cement blocks. The tires were gone. The battery had been lifted out from under the hood too.

It was then he started to cry. It wasn't only about the car and the summer job he was supposed to get to. It was because I had promised him something.

I had said I would come back. He knew then that what I said to him that day at the pool wasn't true. He was left alone on the path my parents had placed us on.

Now his letter was in my hand, and I was crying. I had left him once again when we came to Israel. Although he had been to Europe on business from time to time, he would not come here.

I think he has an aversion to Israel as my mother did. So except for Shmulik who was born in America, Rob never knew my children at all.

He met my three youngest children for the first time when I brought them to America to see my father before he died. He met Estie again when she visited last summer. He saw Shmulik, after twenty-three years, when Shmulik went to New York this year. He has never seen Yossi.

I read on. What we have lived through was worth something in his eyes! He asked me, "How is it humanly possible to live with terrorism day in and day out?"

My children dashed to the computer to write him e-mails. They want so much to have a deep connection with him. They would love for him to marry, to come to Israel, to have children, cousins a generation younger than they. To have a real family in Israel, not just us.

Yehoshua wrote him that he should move here. Estie and Shmulik wrote him to be strong, and he would heal.

I wonder if this will bring us together and make us close again?

Tonight, when I went to sleep, I kept thinking about how to answer Rob. How *do* we live with terrorism?

One way is through faith that God is behind it all. But for those who have lost family, faith in God is not always enough to cope with the pain that worsens as the beloved are missed more and more each passing day. The bereaved families often go to one of the great rabbis and Kabalists living in Israel. There they are told that when the Messiah comes their loved ones will be resurrected. When the Temple is rebuilt, they will be reunited in joy.

But this belief in the resurrection of the dead has caused confusion in children who have lost parents.

"Mommy, whose baby is that in you?" a little girl asked her

mother who had finally remarried. "Is it this daddy's or the daddy that is going to come with the *Messiach*?"

Frank lives with it because he simply has no fear. This seems to be a result of his injury. Because he survived an assault with a large rock that went through his car window and into his face, he believes everything will always be all right.

And me, what about me? I have crossed the point of no return. This is where I live.

September 28

Both Estie and I are trying to ignore the screaming, the whistling of mobs, the gunfire, the grenades, the street battles between the army and the Arabs. They have been going on all day. Estie and I have so much we want to discuss. But we do not want to discuss the Intifada. She must plan her future. I want to help her if I can.

The army has given her a week's vacation so that she can begin to put her life together as a civilian. Next week, after twenty months of duty, Estie finishes her service.

We're preparing together for Shabbat; I'm rolling out the pizzas, she's grating the cheese.

"It wasn't as bad as this when I was in Hebron."

"It *has* gotten worse," I confessed.

She went to the window and closed it.

"I'm leaving all authority now, do you understand, Ema?

Do you know what that means? I don't know if *I* know what that means."

"But we'll always be your parents!"

"I won't be living at home. I know I never will be under your roof again in the same way as before."

"Don't say that."

"It's true."

"Why not start university in Jerusalem in the fall? Then at least you'll have a framework and you'll be close to home."

"No, I need the time to think and breathe. I want to finish my matriculation exam in math. I need to work so that I can travel next year.

"Remember what the medic told me? He said I have to get out of Israel. I've decided to go to America for a while."

"But it's dangerous in America now, Estie!"

She laughs at me. The Arabs in Hebron are on the streets screaming, "Death to America and Israel! Long live Osama bin Laden!" The Arabs who don't have guns are throwing stones and bottles at soldiers. Now more sirens are wailing.

I raise my voice. "But Estie! You'll be an old lady by the time you decide to go to college. How will you meet someone your age to marry?"

"Ema, when did you marry?"

"Twenty-six."

"See? I have time."

"But it's not the same. In Israel there are more girls than boys."

"Because of all our soldier boys who die?"

Our mood changes. Shmulik and Yossi are reserve soldiers

now. Both will do their duty in Judea and Samaria. Yehoshua will be drafted next year. The worry is there. Always the worry, gnawing away at the back of our minds.

"Estie, it's not only that. Kids get married young here. There simply won't be any boys left for you! Look, you're having your twentieth birthday next week!"

And the Arabs are on the streets celebrating. They are celebrating the symmetry, the awful symmetry, that has bracketed our lives. By their reckoning, one year of terror.

October 3

Several thousand Israelis came here to the Cave of the Matriarchs and Patriarchs for the Sukkoth celebrations in spite of the escalation of violence. In the Torah there is a commandment to make the pilgrimage to the Holy Temple in Jerusalem with a lamb or goat to sacrifice. Because there isn't a Holy Temple, Hebron has become one of the favorite pilgrimages for Sukkoth.

Every year the Hebron Jewish community brings people in from all over the country in bulletproof buses. Outside the Cave of the Matriarchs and Patriarchs they set up a huge booth roofed with palm branches. Only in such a booth can a Jew eat for the entire week of Sukkoth.

Everyone picnics. Rabbis and prominent settlers speak about the importance of Hebron to the Jewish nation. Bands play. Kids sell drinks and books about the pogrom in Hebron.

People greet long-lost friends. Men dance in their circles and women in theirs. Buses keep coming. Is it possible so many Jewish pilgrims can fit into the plaza in front of the Cave?

So many soldiers, so many police. There was even a netting of synthetic camouflage leaves surrounding the Hebron festival so that snipers from the hilltop of Abu Sneineh wouldn't be able to take aim. They could just take potshots.

People thought they were hearing firecrackers as if on Independence Day. There was so much noise from the band, and people were dancing. It took several minutes to realize what had happened. They didn't see that two women had fallen on the stairs, and were crying, "I've been shot!"

October 4

Feiga, mother of five, was hit in the chest and abdomen. A young woman named Hadassah was shot in the leg. Feiga is in serious condition. Hadassah is being treated for her wound and trauma.

Yet today thousands upon thousands came once again for the Sukkoth festival in Hebron to show the Arabs that *Am Yisrael Hai!*—the Children of Israel are alive and well.

October 9

Finally, finally the IDF went into Abu Sneineh to wipe out the terrorist installations. And they did not retreat when they'd finished. The army did this in retaliation for the shooting of Feiga and Hadassah outside the Cave.

Two nights ago, hearing a noise like an airplane scraping against the ground with its engines fully revved, we ran to our usual lookout point on the lawn. One father came out holding his little son's hand. With his free arm he pointed. "That's a tank. Nothing can stand against an Israeli tank."

It was making its way up the street, the pavement crunching beneath its tracks.

"Is it going to kill the Arabs?" the little boy asked.

"It's going to protect us so they won't kill us anymore."

"How come they kill us, Aba?"

"Because they want Israel."

"Is Israel ours, Aba?"

"Of course. Didn't Abraham and Sarah stand just where we're standing now?"

"Did they see the tank too?"

A long time afterward we saw the tank crawling up the steep hill. At the top was perched the Arab school which was transferred from Palestinian to Israeli control and back again with every cease-fire or breach of it.

The father stood straight as if he were saluting a flag. I felt more confidence too. We went back into the house and shortly thereafter went to sleep.

This morning, Simchath Torah, Frank and I were sitting on the ledge overlooking the road to Hebron when a man came up to us.

"*Hag Samech.* It's a great holiday. Mazel tov."

"For what?"

"Don't you see the Israeli flags flying on Abu Sneineh?"

How had we not noticed them? One was furling on the shelled-out building we had seen tanks hit once before. The other one crowned what had been a multilevel villa but was now only a one-story house caving into itself.

The mood of people who began to gather on the lawn was one of elation. Their prayers had been answered. Each and every one of us could now get back to the business of leading normal lives.

True, the Americans had started bombing Afghanistan the same day we had retaken Abu Sneineh. But Afghanistan was far away.

The long year of terror was over—at least in Hebron.

October 12

Miriam is in a whirling tizzy. I suppose it's her way of letting off steam. Sometimes she leaves school early, hitchhikes to the Hebron Hills, then waits for someone to drive her to the outpost where Yossi lives. Yossi is usually not at home, so she finds someone to saddle up a horse for her, and she goes galloping down the dirt road to the ruins of the ancient city of Sussya.

Although we tell her that she must not do this because it is dangerous, she says, "Nobody understands me. If you did, you'd know why I have to do this."

She is so impudent that Frank refuses to talk to her. And she doesn't care. She refuses to speak to him. The war outside has stopped. Inside the cold war has begun.

Yossi, Adi, and Shachar pop in all the time now. Morning, evening, or late at night, I never know. All of a sudden the door opens and I see a bundle pushing its way through. In the bundle is Shachar. Yossi is holding his arms out, and Adi is behind him, pregnant, expecting another baby.

Yossi puts Shachar on the floor, and she begins to crawl around the living room followed by our dog, Tagar, who is waiting for an opportune moment. Soon I notice that Tagar has retired happily to her corner and is chewing on Shachar's pacifier. Adi gets upset. She is unused to dogs and always wants me to tie Tagar up. But we tell her that our children grew up with a dog and that Shachar should too.

Sometimes, if Adi insists, I do tie her up to keep peace in the house. Then Tagar whines and barks. Not much peace, but it is happy commotion at least.

Estie scoops Shachar up, enjoying her last days with her. Estie is moving away from here, as far away as you can get and remain in Israel. To Eilat on the southernmost tip of Israel, on the Red Sea. With hot sun all year round and beautiful beaches, it is a resort town where people don't worry about the Intifada at all.

She has just signed on for a year's position as a shift manager for a pizza franchise. She'll be given a room in a beautiful villa and a very good salary. Once a month she'll be able to come home for Shabbat. She starts next week.

And I have started teaching at the University in Beer Sheba, my first position teaching college students.

I spent the entire summer designing and researching the course and creating a "reader" with appropriate texts. Now I am writing the lectures, trying to tie these many elements together. This has absorbed all my energy.

Yesterday was my first day. I was so scared! I fasted, I did yoga, meditated, and prayed the entire morning and afternoon. I wanted to be so good. I wanted them to like me. I wanted the Muse to be with me. As I had been inspired by Abraham, Moses, and Elijah, I wanted to inspire my students.

But suddenly, in the middle of the class, I saw white. I couldn't remember what I wanted to say! I stuttered, my voice cracked and all confidence drained out of me.

Oh, God, I thought. Just help me get through this one class, never mind a whole semester! I got hold of myself, but still I was tense.

Thank God there are only ten students in my class. Quite a few Americans who had already arrived for the Overseas Program were called back home. With the outbreak of the war in Afghanistan, their parents were frightened that there might be repercussions here. A few students who were supposed to arrive never did because their parents didn't want them flying. Then, with the threat of anthrax spores spreading in mail in the United States, they wanted their children near.

My children want me near, but I will so often be out of the house and coming home late at night. Two days a week at the University and my teaching in Jerusalem. As I have for years, I go from house to house teaching English to schoolchildren. Fridays I go early in the morning to learn yoga with Dina, my teacher, my guru. I am also beginning my second year toward my master's degree in foreign literature, and I must begin work on my thesis.

Miriam is complaining bitterly that I will never be home. I try to explain that yoga gives me the spiritual strength I need to be strong for *them*.

At least I don't have to worry about Frank on the roads. I made him take an apartment in Beer Sheba, where he spends a few nights a week. This gives me the inner quiet I need to do all the work I must do.

Although the many blessings that came from heaven when the skies opened seem to have been transformed into a frenzy, I remember something that my good friend Laura once read to me. "If you're not thankful for every little thing you have, God won't give you anything bigger. God gives only to the grateful."

I am grateful for the frenzy. We Leavitts are all alive.

Please, God. Please.

October 14

The roads that were blocked with mounds of dirt have re-opened. The mounds have been plowed away, and Arab vehicles are flowing through. On the bus to Jerusalem today I looked for the reassuring presence of our soldiers on roads that lead into Hebron. My confidence, which fluctuates with every change in government policy, began to ebb.

The bus driver turned up the radio so that passengers could hear the news. It was as I feared. Prime Minister Sharon agreed once again to ease up on the closures around Arab cities so that the Arabs too can resume a normal life.

"Turn the radio up louder!" passengers called out.

Sharon and his security cabinet decided to pull back from Abu Sneineh and relinquish control to Colonel Jibril Rajoub!

"Rajoub promised that he personally would make sure no shots would ever be fired from Abu Sneineh into the Jewish neighborhoods in Hebron," Sharon said.

The very same Rajoub that the CIA had backed to take over Hebron? He was an avowed hater of Jews and had softened his position only on documents that American agents had asked him to sign.

I looked around the bus. One man bent his head lower over the holy book he was studying. A woman took out her Book of Psalms and began reciting them. I closed my eyes and began to do deep and mindful breathing.

October 15

Chaos again like before Creation. Sometimes I wonder if the Hassidic Jews aren't right. Where I live, the religious people believe that the Third Holy Temple will never be destroyed. On the other hand, many Hassidic Jews believe that it should never be rebuilt!

They believe that only in the world to come, when the Messiah descends on the wings of an eagle, should Israeli nationhood be revived.

What a mess we're making, what a mess.

In Hebron today the Jewish residents stormed up to Abu Sneineh in order to make Sharon change his mind. They say they will not put their lives in Rajoub's hands and that the Israeli army must protect them. Estie's friends from the army said the settlers have put the soldiers in a terrible position. If Arabs open fire on them, the army will not be able to retaliate because the settlers will be in between them.

And now Ariel Sharon's government may fall. Two of the right-wing parties that make up his coalition have threatened to pull out of his government because of the withdrawal from Abu Sneineh. The most prominent member of these parties is Rehavam Ze'evi, also known as Ghandi. He is minister of tourism.

He and another minister have handed in resignations which will take effect in two days unless either Sharon reverses his decision or Shimon Peres quits.

If Sharon's government falls it will be the second government to fall within eight months! Such instability certainly does not strengthen this country or give us a feeling of security. Who can lead this nation now?

October 17

The harbinger of evil rang at 7:40 this morning. Two hours earlier, Frank had helped Estie onto the bus with all her bags. She was on her way to her new life in Eilat. He had gone back to bed. I had gotten up to get Miriam off to school.

Shmulik was on the phone from Jerusalem. "Did you hear? Gandhi was shot at the Hyatt Hotel!"

Rehavam Ze'evi was known to most Israelis as Gandhi because he once dressed up at a Purim party as the Indian leader.

But he was known differently to Frank and me.

When we were still new in Hebron, Frank read about Gandhi's intention to create a new political party which advocated the transfer of Arabs living in Israel to Arab countries. Writing to him to offer his help, Frank became one of the activists who helped create the party called *Moledet*, "My Homeland."

When Frank was injured as he was driving home one afternoon in 1990, Gandhi and his wife Yael were among the first people to arrive at Hadassah Hospital in Jerusalem. They stayed with me in the emergency room for five hours until Frank was taken into the operating room to have the broken bones of his face repaired.

I was sure they would go home then. But even then they stayed.

"Go home. Get some sleep," I said again and again. Yael answered by holding my hand, Gandhi by getting up once again to stand vigil at the doors of the operating room.

I couldn't eat. I couldn't drink. Gandhi would get me a glass of water and make me sip that.

Eleven hours later, when the surgeons came out in their masks and slippers to say that Frank was alive and that the operation had been a success, only then did they take leave of me.

This morning, more than a decade later, in the same emergency room where he waited with me, in the same operating theater, Rehavam Ze'evi was pronounced dead of a bullet wound in the neck. An Arab gunman who had checked into the hotel as a guest assassinated Gandhi as he returned to his room from breakfast.

He had so much on his mind, so much in his heart. Perhaps that is why he didn't see the danger coming. He refused bodyguards, arguing that if he should have them then all Israelis should have them. Who was he to have special protection? He had been staying at the Hyatt Hotel for some time, even though it is in East Jerusalem.

"But Jerusalem cannot be divided. It belongs to the Jewish nation forever. That is why I will continue to stay at the Hyatt," he said.

On this day, which was supposed to be the day of Estie's entrance into a new life, she called us from the bus on her cell phone to cry with us. She remembered how, over the years after Frank's injury, Gandhi would write to us and we to him.

And though the leftists here hate him for his hawkish views, and some right-wingers call him a dictator, Estie knew, as we knew, that beneath the militant and shrewd politician was a caring man who felt the pain of Israel and each and every one of her people. For us, he was the man who stood by our sides during the worst hours of our lives.

Ariel Sharon has threatened Yasir Arafat. If Arafat doesn't hand over Gandhi's assassins, Israel will take very strong measures against the Palestinian Authority. But this will not bring Gandhi—friend, father, husband, and grandfather—back to life.

Why didn't the country listen to him? He always said we could not survive with the Arabs in our midst!

October 23

It wasn't because the Arabs were shooting from Bait Jala that I got stranded in Jerusalem last night. In fact the IDF has gone into Bait Jala and Bethlehem because of Arafat's failure to hand over Gandhi's assassins. And all around the West Bank our army has made a siege of Arab villages.

But last night, in the center of Jerusalem, there was a huge rally organized by the right-wing parties. At first it was planned as a protest against Sharon's fluctuating policy on terrorism. But when Sharon launched an offensive against the Palestinian Authority, the massive rally became one of solidarity.

I went to teach, oblivious to the fact that the organizers of the rally had not hired enough buses. So beginning at 9 p.m. I stood at the bus stop and watched the armored bus to Kiriat Arba pass me by hourly, packed. A new regulation states that all passengers on buses into the territories must have a seat. I stood at the bus stop until midnight with some protesters still holding their placards.

The placards did not say, NO ARABS! NO ATTACKS! Those slogans were outlawed by the Israeli government's adviser for legal affairs as racist. Instead the placards read: THE TWINS— ARAFAT AND BIN LADEN! BURY OSLO! NOT US!

November 3

I don't want to see, hear, or write anything disagreeable. I have put the diary aside, saving it for good things only. Sorrow is so very draining.

And fear is even worse. Knowing that statistically the chances are good that either you, someone in your family, or one person you know . . .

I remind myself of what David the Psalmist wrote:

Thou shalt not be afraid for the terror by night;
nor for the arrow that flieth by day . . .
A thousand shall fall at thy side,
and ten thousand at thy right hand;
but it shall not come near thee . . .

For he shall give his angels charge over thee,
to keep thee in all thy ways.

I remind myself of what our friend Yossi Sharvit told us after Arabs shot so many bullets into his car that it looked like a sieve. "All of a sudden I felt myself become as thin as a piece of paper. I knew I was safe, and all the bullets just kept going by."

Frank told me that one of the masters of aikido felt this protected space too. As an officer during World War II, he promised his soldiers that such weak things as bullets could not hurt them. And though he led them into enemy fire many times, it was as he promised. Not a soldier of his was ever touched.

It is this *believing* that nothing will happen . . .

Didn't Jesus the Jew say, "You could move mountains, if only you would believe"?

Sometimes I believe, I believe so strongly. I feel this light in every cell of my body, from my marrow to my skin. This light, this angel on my shoulder.

I hurry past newspaper stands. I do not look because pain would slow me down. With my schoolbooks on my back, I just keep walking up and down, up and down Jerusalem's many little mountains. I know every shortcut, every path, every street from one neighborhood of this city to another. Parks I used to write in, before my teaching day began. Coffee shops I used to dream in—if only I could sell enough books, I would buy a gardened house in Jerusalem.

There are high points where, if I looked east, I could see the walls of the Old City. Until the 1860s Jerusalem existed only behind those fortified walls.

It was Moses Montefiore, the British nobleman of Jewish birth, who encouraged the Jews of Palestine to leave the Old City and their ghetto mind-set when he financed the first neighborhoods outside the fortified walls. At first the Jews were so frightened to live there, he had to pay them to go there each day. But at night they went running back behind the walls of the Old City.

Not until World War I, when a wave of secular Jews immigrated to Israel, were those neighborhoods filled and new neighborhoods built in the west. There the new Jerusalem began to grow.

After the Holocaust, acknowledging the Jewish people's need for a country of their own, the United Nations made a resolution endorsing the division of Palestine into two states, one for the Arabs and one for the Jews.

In 1948 the Jews of Palestine declared Israel an independent state. The Arabs of Palestine, supported by Lebanon, Syria, Iraq, Jordan, and Egypt immediately declared war. The Gaza Strip was taken by Egypt. The Golan Heights were taken by Syria. Judea and Samaria were taken by Jordan, as was the Old City of Jerusalem.

The cease-fire that brought the war to an end divided the city. All of East Jerusalem, including the Old City with the Wailing Wall and the Temple Mount, went to Jordan. West Jerusalem, with its new neighborhoods, went to Israel.

"Jerusalem is our ancient and new capital!" David Ben-Gurion, the first prime minister of Israel declared.

Israel's capital remained divided until the Six-Day War in 1967. When the Israeli army entered Jordanian East Jerusalem, and conquered it, Jewish soldiers wept at the Wailing Wall.

Since then, every Israeli government has declared that an undivided Jerusalem will be the capital of Israel for eternity. This has given the people of Jerusalem a confidence and sense of security that we who live in disputed territory have never had.

Often my pupils' parents would say to me, "How can you live there?"

I didn't know what to say. Maybe all of Israel *does* belong to the Jews for eternity, but was living in disputed territory worth the price it exacted?

My Jerusalem pupils always seemed to be more carefree than my own children. More able to concentrate. They had none of the complexes that come from living outside "politically correct" boundaries—the feeling of being disliked, of being a pariah. They had none of the stress caused by being a rope in a game of political tug-of-war.

Most of my pupils loved the Arabs. They were all young activists for the left-wing parties. The Intifada was far away from them. They hadn't known any victims of the "Peace." During the peace negotiations the sound of sirens coming from the motorcade of limousines on their way to or from the stately King David Hotel did not make them go dry in the mouth with fear.

The name Madeline Albright didn't give them goose bumps. When President Clinton came to Jerusalem and many of the city streets were closed for several days, they weren't made sleepless by the implications.

None of the fallout from the peace accords contaminated their lives. Jerusalem was a healthy city with mountain upon mountain of olive trees; old neighborhoods of pink stone; ancient history underfoot and appearing around every corner. Children walked about with their friends anywhere, anytime and hung out on the pedestrian mall in the center of the city, weaving in and out among the tourists who flocked to the city.

Now when I walk up the steps to the apartment buildings, the mothers greet me with sighs.

"When is this going to end?

"Every day. It can make you crazy. I don't even want to hear it. I shut off the radio and the television. There was another one just now."

"What? What happened?"

"I don't know. An Egged bus at the French Hill junction. Arabs opened fire."

I closed my eyes. How many times had my boys, and even Miriam, stood at that junction hitchhiking to Yossi's at Ittamar.

"Was anybody killed?"

"What do you think, June? It's 4:30 in the afternoon. Every bus is full of school kids on their way home. We can't live with the Arabs. I wanted to give them their own country so I would never have to see them. You know why I'm a leftist who wanted the peace? Because I can't stomach them. Can I make you a cup of tea?"

I sit down with her daughter. We do not say anything. We do not speak of these things.

Just last month, in this quiet neighborhood, a car bomb

went off down the street. Soon after that, in the industrial area near here, an Arab with a pistol opened fire on everyone, just like that.

My pupil says, "I'm having a test in English on present progressive and present simple. Can we go over it again?"

I settle back in the chair and repeat an exercise. "What are you doing *now*?"

"I learn English with June now."

"No. I *am* learning English."

"Are you having a good time *now*?"

"Sometimes."

"Do you have a good time every day?"

"I used to. But now we can't go anywhere anymore. There used to be *things* sometimes. Now there are *things* every day. So after school we come straight home and stay inside. It's boring."

I think migrating birds sense these *things*.

Half a billion migrate over Israel twice a year on their way to and from Africa. And many of them would go by way of this city. Ornithologists could never understand why flocks of storks, ducks, pelicans, and hawks would make so many twirling trails and rainbows in the skies over Jerusalem.

But they don't come here anymore. Not in those numbers anyway.

November 7

Why? Everyone is asking. After thousands of years of *things*, what's all this now?

Rabbis are on the radio calling for secular Jews to return to God and the fulfillment of the 613 commandments that God has given them. The Messiah is in the wings just waiting for the Jews to ready themselves for him. He will make a grand feast. Do you want to be on the inside or the outside?

Secular men are putting on skullcaps as the religious ones do and running to the synagogues. Others are taking their skull caps off, flocking to India and the Far East to search for their answers.

This is an odd phenomenon in Israel. For the Israelites gave the world the Bible, and all answers were said to have been within it. What was "without" was not clean. This is the land where the biblical injunction against fortune-tellers and soothsayers still holds, thousands of years after King Saul put them to the sword.

This is the land where everything not quite understood is condemned as *avoda zara,* the worshipping of strange gods. Imprinted deep in the Jewish mind is the memory of Moses smashing the tablets of the Covenant because the Jews had sought salvation elsewhere.

Now there are Russians who lay on stones and crystals, and men and women who can release the pain of trauma through a touch. Many can take you back to past lives so that you know what spiritual error you have come to earth to remedy. Uta, a

German convert to Judaism, told me she would regress me to find out why my husband and I continue to live in Kiriat Arba-Hebron, even though for twenty years we have tried to move.

There are women who work with lead to get rid of the evil eye. Many work with the pendulum after several rabbis decided that the pendulum was permissible under Jewish law as long as one didn't ask about the future.

There is the rabbi's son who follows the Sufi path. There are rabbis who read fingernails and through them prescribe a *tikun*, a correction for the soul. There are those who open a holy book at random and know that the words they find before their eyes have been selected for them by divine providence.

Oh Israelites, you must unite! Remember the words of the prophets of old who foretold the destruction of the Holy Temple because Jew fought with Jew; North African Jewry with Western European Jewry; religious Zionists with Hassidic Jews; those on the left with those on the right.

Some look to the stars for answers. A woman in my yoga class who had been in favor of the "Peace" asked, "Why is this happening to us? What is the karma of the Jews?"

To which someone answered, "Mercury is out of line. It is in retrograde—moving backward through the zodiac. That is why things have been bad. Things will get better soon."

In a sense they are better. Ariel Sharon is closing in on known terrorists. In Hebron last week an attack helicopter fired a missile at the killer of our neighbor Danny Vargas. For years, the GSS knew where Jamil Jadala was living but was hesitant to act. The murderer of Sarit Amrani, the young mother who left behind three babies and a critically injured husband, was himself assassinated.

And just now, Yossi walked in. "Finally we killed the murderer of Dov Dribben!" For the past four years my boys have known exactly who had planned Dov's murder—Isa Dababase. They knew as well as the GSS that he lived a hero's life in the village of Chirbat Karmel in the Hebron Hills.

On his communications radio, Yossi heard that a special unit of soldiers dressed as Arabs had entered Chirbat Karmel. They were met by villagers wielding knives and clubs but overcame them. When they approached the murderer's house, Isa Dababase came out firing his pistol and was gunned down. He died just as Dov had, in dust and blood.

And eye for an eye. A life for a life.

November 9

Is there a thread that ties my Jerusalem life to my life in Kiriat Arba? Is it the same thread that winds on to Beer Sheba where I teach at the University?

If going to Jerusalem was like going to another state, going to Beer Sheba was like going to another country. Israel is a tiny country, and yet the changes from one locality to another can be drastic.

I knew how my husband had suffered from going through

these changes daily. I knew that when he got to Beer Sheba he would take off his sweater and put on a short-sleeved shirt. There it was desert, and here lush from plentiful winter rain.

But it wasn't only the difference in geography and climate that caused suffering. It was the people there. The forces that had formed them, had not formed him.

Beer Sheba is known only as the place where Abraham and Sarah went during the winter when they couldn't bear the Hebron cold. There they found a well from which Beer Sheba takes its name.

How unlike Jerusalem and Hebron, where the earth has been formed from bones and blood. The desert is stark. It cleanses the mind and does not awaken painful memories.

Frank's colleagues, especially in the Liberal Arts faculty, before he moved to the medical school, would say to him, "It's because of you we have troubles with the Arabs! You took their homes! You chased them off their land! Because of you, soldiers must serve in the Territories! Because of you we have had to rule over the Palestinian people who don't want us to rule them!

"You have no right to live in the territories conquered during the Six-Day War. Settlers like you in Judea, Samaria, and the Gaza Strip are Nazis!"

They voted in Yitzhak Rabin on the "Territories for Peace" platform. After he was killed, they voted in Ehud Barak on the same platform. It was a shock when they voted in the right-wing Ariel Sharon.

Terrorism, they believed, had been the legitimate expression of an oppressed people when it was perpetrated in the "Occupied Territories." But for the past year it has spread all over Israel.

By the time I began traveling with Frank to Beer Sheba, no one was shouting, "Nazi settler!" Rather, I was met with, "June, I can't believe you made the trip from Kiriat Arba to here! Do you do it every day? Isn't it dangerous? You know, I was worrying about you when I heard about the shootings!"

I felt a thin thread being spun in my fingers. A thread uniting the people in this discordant country as it united the discordant parts of my self.

This does not mean that I can speak openly to my neighbors in Kiriat Arba, Hebron, about the Gospel of Matthew, a text I was teaching as part of my course on spirituality. Christianity is the worship of strange gods. If my neighbors could, they would put me to the sword or in *herem*—isolate me from the community.

Nor does it mean that I can speak outside my classroom to anyone in Beer Sheba about the spiritual power that emanates from the Cave of the Patriarchs and Matriarchs, only 150 yards from our tiny apartment.

So the feeling of living at a distance still remains. The loneliness is with me still. Not belonging. Neither there. Nor here.

Last night the army and police set up roadblocks in the city of Beer Sheba. We used to get to such roadblocks only as we entered the "Occupied Territories." But last night, while still in Beer Sheba, we were held up in a traffic jam as soldiers and police inspected each car.

We knew what this meant. Beer Sheba, once thought to be one of the safest places in Israel, was no longer safe. There were serious warnings of an imminent attack in the city. Everyone knows that the GSS has a network of informers in the Arab sectors. This network has weakened as Arabs suspected of ties with Israelis have been tortured, then hung on electric poles, nooses around their bloodied necks and left to dangle for days. In this case, though, one informer must have handed over very specific information. Otherwise there would not have been this dragnet.

We got through after one hour, only to be held up as we got to the Hebron Hills. The soldiers who stopped us at a road-block poked their heads into the car after Frank rolled down the window. "The road is closed. You'll have to wait here."

"What happened?"

They replied, "On the road you just came from, a car was just now shot at. Must have been the car right behind you. No one was injured."

"But if the shooting was behind us, why can't we drive ahead?"

The soldiers didn't answer. They didn't want to frighten me. Frank said, "The gunmen are still in the hills."

When we got home so late, my children were angry. Not at the Arabs for shooting at a car and delaying us, but at Frank and me.

More particularly me. For the past few weeks, I have been going full speed. I am often away in Beer Sheba or in Jerusalem teaching. When I'm at home, I'm trying to meet a publisher's deadline.

My mind and energy have been so consumed that I am aloof even with my own family. Frank has felt the brunt of my neglect. One of my children broke down crying, "I want a mother when I get home!" Another child of mine just said to me, "You're missing all the joy of having a family!"

Our dog is also feeling neglected. I no longer bicycle with her running after me. Her eyes look sad.

I am being pulled this way and that. The delicate thread in my hands is breaking.

December 1

In preparing my classes on the Buddha (which I dare not tell my religious children about) I came across this quotation from an ancient text:

Life in the home is indeed attended by a great many faults and calamities.

This is so true that sometimes I imagine myself in the quiet of a monastery, a place without my children's anger, without their expectations that I am unable to fulfill.

My soul is yearning to be elsewhere, not rushing from Beer Sheba to Jerusalem under enemy fire, trying to make a living.

What would happen if I voluntarily gave up family life and went to live a life of contemplation on a quiet mountaintop somewhere? Would I lose the fear of losing them, and thereby be free of fear? I wish myself to a place of Stillness and Tranquility of Mind.

December 2

In the past day forty people have been killed in a wave of attacks all over the country.

On Saturday night the pedestrian mall in the heart of Jerusalem was filled with teenagers who had defied their parents cry of "Do not go there! It's dangerous!"

They went there to laugh, to forget, to show they would not give in to terror. Among the crowds of youth, two suicide bombers blew themselves up in a choreographed attack.

Shocked teenagers, running from the first bomber's deadly explosion, ran right into the second one. Just as medics came running from a nearby hospital, a car bomb exploded and injured some of them.

One hundred seventy people were injured last night in the pedestrian Mall bombings. Eleven were killed.

Today at noon, on a crowded bus in Haifa, a suicide bomber turned himself and the bus into a fiery rocket which soared from the road onto a sidewalk.

So far ten bodies have been identified from the bus explosion. The identification is difficult. DNA sampling will have to be used. Eighty-two injured. Fifteen believed killed.

Israel has struck hard at the PLO. Our air force bombed Arafat's helicopter at the airport in Gaza and hit his home with rockets. His headquarters in Ramallah were also targeted.

Now the doctrinal dispute is flaming once again. In the cabinet the Labor party members walked out. They say there is not a trinity. There are only two.

The right-wing members of the government say there *is* a trinity: Arafat's Palestinian Liberation Organization *and* Hamas *and* the Islamic Jihad—*three* terrorist organizations that aim at Israel's destruction.

The Labor party says no, Arafat's PLO is not one of them. He is a partner in peace.

The right wing says, No, there is a trinity. A trinity of terror.

December 6

I could not write of this before. It was too painful.

My classes at the University went well as long as we stayed within the parameters of Judaism. When we got to the Christian scriptures I felt as though I was losing my authority. The pupils kept turning to a Catholic girl in the class for answers to their questions. By the time we got to Buddhism, a brilliant but troublesome boy in the class asked if he could take over the class during our reading of *Siddhartha*.

I agreed, and the class went beautifully. Inspired by Hermann Hesse's seeker, everyone started opening up and speaking of their own spiritual searches. Then, just as Siddhartha had said to his teacher, my students said that spirituality cannot be learned from a teacher. It is life and the search for one's destiny that teaches it.

"I appreciate your desire to seek the truth," I finally commented at the end. "But where do I, as your teacher, fit into this?"

"You do not fit in," they answered. "Not as a teacher. Your experiences are no more valid than ours."

I cried on the way home with Frank. Trying to comfort me, he said, "June, the first commandment of teaching is, 'Thou shalt not lose control of thy class.' You just did. It will be very hard to get it back."

At home I closed myself in my room and wept. I wrote in my diary. I threw the tarot which showed that deep forces were at play in my class. The Magician at the center showed that I had channeled great powers into the classroom. The overturned Chariot showed I had lost control of them. What will be the outcome? Three people dancing comforted me. Cups held water that flowed.

I prayed to be shown how to grow from this experience, how to flow with the class so that we would all be made wiser and better.

When I went into class two days later, I could not speak. Instead, I read what I had written in my diary:

"We did an experiment with Greek democracy. And like Socrates I was given poison to drink.

"Like the children left alone on their own to rule the island on which they find themselves, they vote to put the adults to death. . . .

"Like Gorbachev, who opened the Soviet Union and found he was no longer ruler of a Union. . . .

"This is how I feel. Yet I did not drink the poison. You did not kill me. I am still alive. And because you have indeed chosen to go to University, and not to roam the world as mendicants with begging bowls, and because you are in my class, I will remain your teacher until the end of the semester. Then you can dispense with all teachers if you like. Until that time it is my responsibility to teach you what I know, and to give you the tools of understanding you may need on your journeys.

"And do not be put off by the few wrinkles I have on my face. Do not take my lack of youthful vigor to mean that I haven't thrown more lives away than you have lived in order to search.

"That I haven't dismantled worlds and myself one thousand times. You said two days ago, 'Adults? What can they teach us? We've had more experiences than them!'

"I don't know if that's true. I want you to know something about me. It's an important part of my life and my search. I withheld it, but I feel now, as the course is ending, that I want to lay things on the table."

I put the books I had written on the table. My pupils were shocked. They didn't know.

"Through writing I search for meaning and form in chaos. I live in Kiriat Arba, Hebron. Aside from my children, these are the products of my life."

Then my pupils gathered around me, moving from the far end of the seminar table. "Why did you keep yourself hidden!

"We learned nothing from your lectures! All the dates, all the history meant nothing to us! Tell us about yourself!"

So I told them about destroying the Jewish-American princess within me. And the voice that came to me and told me it was time to leave the Bowery to search for Indians in Vermont.

And meeting Frank there in the woods. The way we took up our journey together and came to Israel. And how Frank encouraged me to write, though I never dreamed I would be writing this diary in Hebron.

"See," I said. "What we think we are searching for, is not what we find. We are pulled through this life, pulled by our destiny."

December 10

Miriam made herself get up from her sickbed in order to perform in her class show—a melodrama about the old *kibbutzim*, fighting the Arabs and dying. But she hammed it up and made everyone laugh. Everyone was in such great need of lightness that she stole the show!

I came home after the show and left her a note on our message board telling her how good she had been. Then I went to bed. When she got home she erased my note and left one in its place.

Dear Ema,

Pleased, pleased with your compliments about my acting. Thank you for coming. Now I know that everything depends on willpower. When we have that, we can do anything. ANYTHING!

Isn't this what the ancient alchemists were searching for? Not how to make lead into gold, but how to transmute darkness into light?

We have all become alchemists in our family. Like the Magician in the tarot deck, we have been given the power to transform pain into perfection.

Recently, when I've been knocked down, though at first I'm dazed and despairing, I take the lesson I must learn from it and then make something good of it.

At the University I was devastated when my students took the class away from me. Having prayed for wisdom, wisdom was granted me. I humbled myself and allowed them to show me and teach me.

January 7, 2002

As if in answer to my prayers, Estie has decided not to spend next year in America but to start college in Israel. But she was just let go from the job she loved in Eilat, the resort town where she was making her home. The American company had to break its contract with her because tourists are simply not coming to Israel.

"Ema, what should I do? Please ask your pendulum! Tell it I don't want to move back to Israel.

"In Eilat," she explained, "people have no idea about the terrorism in the rest of the country. We don't listen to the news. When the radio is on in Eilat, it's only to music. Life is fun here, Ema. No Arabs threaten us!"

"Estie?" I say. "Have you gone to the shore of the Red Sea in the past few days?"

"Why?"

"The *Karine A* is there. You didn't hear?"

I told her that Israeli sea commandos had seized a freighter, the *Karine A,* in the waters off Saudi Arabia and had brought it into the port of Eilat, just down the hill from where she lives.

On board were tons of Katyusha rockets, mortars, anti-tank missiles, mines, explosives, AK-47 assault rifles, and ammunition. The ship was manned by Palestinian naval officers allegedly connected to Yasir Arafat. They deny that the ship's destination was a port in Egypt where the deadly cargo was to be unloaded and then smuggled over the border into Gaza.

"Did you see it, Estie?"

"No, and I don't want to. Ema, please get your pendulum and ask it what I should do!"

I take the teardrop amethyst out of its laminated box and hold it by the chain. I just say "Estie" and "Eilat" and it's already swinging crazily. "Yes."

"Stay there, honey. With all those mortars and assault rifles in Eilat now, you should be pretty safe."

January 18

Life was coming back to normal. We were healing from the past sixteen months, doing the spiritual work of transformation which cannot be done under prolonged stress.

But after two months of relative quiet, the Arab uprising has flared again. I do not mean to say that people haven't been killed in the past two months. Civilians have been slain and soldiers have been murdered, and I have not done them justice.

But now the violent acts against us have resumed with such great fury that we cannot think of anything else or catch our breath to heal.

Yaella Hen, forty-five, mother of two, was shot in the Jerusalem neighborhood of Givat Ze'ev as she pulled out of a gas station. Her seventy-year-old aunt saw two men standing by the side of the road when suddenly they lifted their arms and aimed.

"No, no," she screamed. But they fired anyway.

The American immigrant Avi Boaz had just remarried his wife who was in the terminal stages of cancer; the ceremony took place in the hospice. A few days later she died. Avi got up from sitting *shivah*. Three days later he was killed.

He immigrated from America in the 1960s and worked as an architect near Bethlehem, designing and building homes for Arabs. Arabs were his best friends, his family. He slept in their villages and ate in their houses. He preferred them to Jews. He was sitting in the car with his Arab partner when Palestinian assailants opened fire on him.

Last night, at a Bat Mitzvah celebration in Hadera for a

Russian immigrant girl, a terrorist wearing a heavy coat and cap came running into the wedding hall and began shooting. Six guests were killed, many were injured.

Why are so many people doing yoga, like me? Aikido, like Frank? Learning how to concentrate and control fluctuations of the mind? Why are so many people trying to unite body with soul?

Because we are all searching for that stillness in which prophecy can take root. The medieval Jewish philosopher and poet Rabbi Yehuda Ha Levi proclaimed in his *Book of the Kuzari* that the Jewish nation is a nation of prophets.

Yet I know that prophecy cannot happen where there is sadness. One has to be free from worry, fear, and stress. Soul and body have to be clear and clean. Just look at Jacob our forefather.

When his older sons threw their younger brother, Joseph, into a deep well, and then told Jacob that an animal had clawed him to death, Jacob had no more prophetic visions. Years later, when he was informed that Joseph was alive and flourishing in Egypt, he once again became peaceful in his soul, and the spirit of prophecy returned to him.

So the Intifada not only stamps out lives. It stamps out the ability to create the conditions for prophecy.

January 22

At 2 p.m. today Hamas declared all-out war on Israel.

Two hours later Yehoshua called me on his mobile phone. His voice was muffled and I heard sirens one after another. "I'm all right! There was just a terrorist attack near me!"

"Where? Where are you?"

"Jerusalem," he managed to tell me before his phone went dead.

Immediately I tried calling Shmulik who lives in a dormitory at Hebrew University in Jerusalem. There was no answer.

I tried him on his mobile phone. Thousands of other people were also frantically trying to reach one another on mobile phones. The network had collapsed.

There was nothing to do but turn on the radio and hear that the center of Jerusalem was once again a scene of carnage. A terrorist with an M-16 opened fire at a crowded bus stop on Jaffa Street, just yards away from the Sbarro Restaurant, the site of the suicide bombing in July. Just yards away from the Ben Yehuda pedestrian mall, site of the two suicide bombings last month.

Today at least two people were killed and scores injured.

I called Frank. "Have you heard from Shmulik? He wouldn't be in the center of town now, would he?"

"Of course not. Don't worry. He'll be fine."

An hour later Shmulik called.

January 23

What irony!

One of the two women killed in the attack, Sarah Hamborger, was a survivor of the 1929 Arab pogrom in Hebron. From that experience she learned never to be afraid and she went about Jerusalem without fear.

One of those seriously injured was a nineteen-year-old girl from Chicago who studies at a Jewish seminary in Jerusalem. Although many Americans won't let their children come to Israel now, the Gould family, who love Israel, let Shayna come. Shayna was shot in the chest. She is in critical condition.

Who will come to Jerusalem now?

Stores have been gutted from the explosions. Windows blown out in the attack five days ago were blown out once again. At some shops, windows are still boarded up. Through the cracks you can see the blackened interiors, the twisted metal. If the wind blows you can smell the unmistakable smell of death.

This was the heart of Jerusalem!

In undamaged stores the injured were laid out on stretchers. Among the jeans and sneakers they were given first aid by medics before they were rushed by ambulance to the hospital.

Store owners look woefully out of their shops, their eyes perking up when someone passes. It was bad enough when foreigners stopped coming because their governments put Israel on the list of countries that are too dangerous to visit. But now even Israelis have stopped coming. Israelis who were never before frightened by war and terrorism.

The man who sells the felafel has his chin propped in his hands above all the salads you can stuff into your pita, free! Just down the street, the busy steak restaurant has closed its doors. The sidewalk cafés are lifeless. The faithful still walk around Jerusalem. They believe in God. When it's your turn to die, you die.

They visit the little shrines that have been set up—one near the Sbarro restaurant, one on the mall, one near the bus stop— to lay a bouquet, to light a candle, to say a prayer for Shayna, to utter a Psalm, to stare at the pictures of the slain who are beyond prayer.

At every corner there are soldiers and police. But they have not come to shop or eat. They are positioned to guard the city. They keep watch from rooftops over the nearly empty streets.

Only the elderly seem to walk around.

Oh yes, there are beggars. But they have no money for a pita and felafel now. They rattle only a few agoras in their empty cans. Who will put five shekels in?

Jerusalem has become a war zone. Neither the mayor nor the prime minister say sugary optimistic things any longer. Grimly they admit that the war will heighten. Many more people will be killed; many more will be injured. There's nothing for the people in Jerusalem to do except to buckle in and to know that they are strong and will survive. Jerusalem is their inheritance. It will never perish, nor will the Jewish nation, though other nations rise and fall.

January 27

This morning Miriam had a class trip to the Old City in Jerusalem. I traveled to Jerusalem too, but I gave her our mobile phone.

I was sitting in the library of the American Cultural Center doing research for my master's thesis when the guard at the entrance below turned his radio up so loud that it was impossible to study. At first I was annoyed. But then I heard that word.

"Attack."

Quickly I gathered up my books.

"Where now?" I asked the guard.

"Down the road on Jaffa Street again. Didn't you see the people running?"

I pushed open the thick security door.

There were people scattering on the sidewalk, catching their breath, punching numbers on their cell phones.

Suddenly I remembered. Not only was Shmulik in Jerusalem but Miriam was in Jerusalem too. She had my phone.

"Can I use yours?" I asked the guard.

"Sure," he replied, handing it to me. "But I don't think you'll be able to get through. The lines are overloaded."

It was as he said.

I left to go to a pupil's home. Maybe I could get through on a regular phone. I didn't realize that at the same time I was so worried about my family, my family was in anguish about me. All along the way I saw people whose faces expressed what I was feeling, what my family was feeling. Useless mobile phones in hand. No phone lines. Just the sound of sirens.

January 31

Miriam had to go to the center of Jerusalem to see an eye doctor. Once upon a time I wouldn't have thought twice about it. Throughout high school both Shmulik and Estie traveled to school in Jerusalem every day.

That was then. Now I wonder if there isn't an eye doctor in another city.

On the way to the doctor's office she went with a friend into a clothing store on Jaffa Street to buy a skirt.

"Did you hear the explosion from the attack?" Miriam asked the salesgirl.

"Which one are you talking about?" the salesgirl answered blithely. "I heard them all, and I even managed to be in a few of them. This last time I had luck. So many people injured, some really badly. One man was killed. And me, not a scratch. This time my ears aren't even ringing. I was crossing the street, right there you see, and this *woman* suddenly blew herself up right in front of me."

Yes, the suicide bomber was a woman.

Although strategically it makes sense—Arab women are subjected to less frisking by the IDF and police—it took security investigators six days to reach the conclusion that hers was a suicide mission and not a bomb that exploded prematurely as she carried it to its destination.

The fact that a woman was used for a suicide mission represents a new phase in terror, a departure from the few laws that keep a space of sanity around our lives. In Vietnam the American soldiers were tortured psychologically because they never had this space. Every peasant, man or woman, was a potential enemy. There was no mental relaxation.

Once upon a time here in Israel, all women were sacrosanct. When we first moved to Hebron, we were told that Arab men would never attack a Jewish woman, and that Arab women would never attack anyone.

But gradually that changed. On many occasions Arab women thrust knives into the backs or bellies of Israeli civilians and soldiers. They planted bombs. After they were given the right to drive, they drove suicide bombers to their targets.

And Jewish women could be attacked, and were. Our friend Sarah Nakshon, the holy woman of Kiriat Arba, was attacked in the Jewish cemetery of Hebron back in the 1980s when she went there to visit the grave of her infant son. Since then many Jewish women have been attacked and killed.

So what has changed? What has removed that protective space of sanity?

Once upon a time the laws of Islam prevented a woman from attaining the highest position that could be reached by a Muslim—becoming a *shahid*, a martyr. That was reserved for their superiors, the men.

172

But in 1995, Eddie Dribben, Dov's father, told us about an incident with an Arab woman in Hebron. So we knew frightening changes were brewing.

With the brass handles of his daggers sticking out of their sheaths and pistols in holsters all over his body, Eddie Dribben was doing his business as usual in an Arab shop. Suddenly an Arab woman entered. She was dressed according to *hijab*, the Islamic code of dress for women. She wore a long drab coat with sleeves that extended to her knuckles. The hem of her coat fell to the toes of her black leather shoes. A large scarf covered her head and neck. Over her face she wore a veil of sheer black chiffon.

She told the shopkeeper she was collecting for Hamas. Eddie was surprised. Religious Islamic women did not go out into the world and speak to strange men. When guests came into their families' homes, they were ushered into a back room where they would not be seen. The Koran says that whenever a woman is alone with a strange man, there is a third with them—the devil.

Now she turned to Eddie. She was studying his body. Rules were flying away fast. She asked in Arabic, "What are all those things on your body?"

"My limbs," Eddie answered in Arabic.

"What if I take them from you?" she teased him.

"Watch how you talk to your elders, sister."

Suddenly she began speaking to him in very good English.

"Where did you get that English, sister?"

If religious Islamic girls went to school at all, it was only for the lower grades, and they were never taught a second language.

"And how come you're talking to me, you being a religious Muslim woman, and me being a man, and a Jewish infidel at that?"

She replied, "Where do you live?"

"Right now, Kiriat Arba," he said. "But I'm moving out to live among your Arab friends. Know the industrial area? I just bought a big factory. I'm going to live in it with my horses. I make saddles and holsters. Why don't you come over and help me set it up? You look like a woman of taste."

He thought he caught a seductive smile under the veil.

A week later, when Eddie tied up his white mare in front of the same Arab shop, the owner came out and motioned him away. "That woman told Hamas that you come here. The next day they paid me a visit. They said if you walked in again, they'd burn my shop to the ground."

So we knew that Islamic fundamentalist women were throwing off their traditional roles. They were getting out of their homes, becoming educated, becoming proficient in English, slowly working their way up to take part in whatever would emerge from the present anarchy.

We did not foresee that kitchen knives would be thrust aside as relics of the Arab woman's former role. The liberated Muslim woman would seize state-of-the-art implements of destruction.

Hamas would declare all-out war on Israel. Arab women could, if they chose, take their heroic places next to their men as equals. They too could attain the highest position in the Islamic world, not as corporate presidents but as martyrs.

The homicidal martyrdom of women signals something

truly frightening—violation of the eternal law that the female brings forth life.

The suicide bomber of Jaffa Street worked for the Red Crescent Emergency Clinic. Dressed in white uniform, she was brought to the heavily guarded intersection by an ambulance. Some say she was a nurse. Others say she was a paramedic.

There is another eternal law this female suicide bomber broke. Healers do not kill. They save.

February 15

Even with my angel on my shoulder, I feel fear creeping in. Is there anyone, no matter how much faith she has, who doesn't worry about her loved ones?

Whoever says they are not frightened is telling a lie. Whoever says they are not deeply concerned for their family is not telling the truth.

Even Frank, who never worries, breathlessly asks, "Is everything all right?" when he calls from Japan.

I blurt out, though I didn't intend to, "No, not at all. There was a terrorist attack in Beer Sheba! Beer Sheba, can you believe it? At lunchtime an Arab went to a crowded eating place and just starting shooting. Two women soldiers were killed.

"Please don't come home, Frank! Things are crazy here. Another Arab woman blew herself up!"

★

Miriam and I are becoming so close. I think she senses that a space has been created by Frank's absence in Japan, and wordlessly she's entered it.

After she finishes her day in school, we prepare meals together, the healthy things she likes. We make a hearty Indian soup. We sauté mustard seeds in hot oil until they pop, then add turmeric, cumin, coriander powder, green squash, and carrots. The mustard seeds release an oil that gives the vegetable soup wonderful, nourishing substance. We have whole-wheat noodles with olive oil and fresh-pressed garlic, and we talk about this and that.

The changes in the eternal laws have dictated changes in my own life. I'm spending more time at home these days. My semester at the University has finished. I am not taking on any additional teaching days in Jerusalem. I want to be a woman and to nurture my children. Although they are nearly grown and the two youngest are almost out the door, it is never too late. When my children said that I was missing all the joy of having a family, I knew they were right.

"Come here," Miriam said the first night Frank was away. She hugged me to her. "I'll be your mother," she said, "all right, my little girl? You're lonesome, a little bit scared? You sleep next to me tonight and I'll take care of you."

I am bathing in the tub of my apartment on the Lower East Side in New York City. One hand is on my abdomen, the other is plunged into the hot water. The bathroom is painted red, and my head is in a whirlpool, gathering up from someplace deep, a terrible anxiety that I have become no more than a hungry artist on the Bowery, inking pictures and poems like Eleanor Rigby's, which no one will see. Perhaps they will find me on the sidewalk years from now, old and shriveled with the bums, a piece of paper clutched in my hand, and on it written: This was my life. This was no game.

Beyond this chaos of my life, there is no immutable substance, no God. Nothing to hold on to. I grip the sides of the tub with both hands. The bath is hot, yet I am shivering. In a panic, I fly out of the water.

Looking for calm, I buy a book that mysteriously appears in front of my eyes on a bookseller's shelf—*Nature's Children* by Juliette de Baraclai-Levi, who lived in the Galilee. I have never heard of this woman since, though allegedly she lived in Israel. No one had heard of her then.

Reading the book, I am inspired. Although Juliette has not written about Indians or teepees, my odd vision comes as an imperative, defying all reason. I must go look for Indians living in teepees.

I had learned in primary school that Indians kidnapped and

killed white settlers, and that Americans had almost annihilated them. Yet now I felt that if only I could find Indians, a spiritual people deeply connected to the earth, I would find wholeness in place of the void. In place of chaos I would find spiritual health and peace.

Six weeks later, walking in the woods of Vermont looking for Indians, I encountered a man. He was not an Indian, and he was holding the hand of a little boy.

"Where am I?" I asked.

"You don't know?" he replied. "So what are you doing here?"

"Looking for Indians. What about you?"

He told me he had taught philosophy at a university in Ohio but that the academic world was too bourgeois, too tied up with the war in Vietnam.

"I'm taking courses at Goddard College on how to use alternate sources of energy for heating and cooking. Then I'm going to homestead on five acres of land I bought in Massachusetts. My name is Frank. This is my son, Benjamin. Are you Jewish?"

Frank didn't know why he asked that. He didn't realize then that the forces that had brought us together in the woods of Vermont would bring us back to our people and nation. But it would take five years.

First we went to live in his woods in Massachusetts, where we built with our own hands a small round wooden house. We felled trees to put in gardens. We lived there two years, drinking water from a pure spring that babbled by our house, eating organic vegetables we had grown, studying philosophy at night by gas lamps. Benjamin lived with us sometimes, sometimes with his mother.

Although we had created a physical Garden of Eden, Frank felt spiritual emptiness. It brought him to a Hassidic rabbi who lived in Amherst, Massachusetts. Gradually Frank became immersed in Hassidic Judaism. Soon I followed.

We taped Hebrew letters on the handlebars of our bicycles (our only means of transportation) and recited the *aleph-beit* as we pedaled along. Soon we could pick out words in the prayers we were learning. One word kept appearing again and again. That word was *Israel*.

The word rolled around in our heads for another two years before we acted on it. Meanwhile we married in a Hassidic wedding and lived in Brooklyn for six months learning how to be Hassidic Jews. Pregnant, with my head now covered, not a hair showing, I wanted to leave Brooklyn. I persuaded Frank that we should set up another homestead, this time in the Catskill Mountains, now as ultra-Orthodox Jews.

Shmulik was born in the Catskills, the first generation of what I thought would be a line of our descendants connected to Mother Earth. The Exile had turned Jews into a people alienated from land; we would change all that. Other observant Jewish families would follow us to the Catskills, and Torah would waft out of the hills as it had in Jerusalem.

While the words *Israel* and *Jerusalem* had burrowed into my consciousness, for Frank they burned. More and more he began to feel that if we hoped to revive our connection to earth, it should be on that piece of land that God had promised the Jewish people.

179

I didn't really want to emigrate to Israel. I thought, well, perhaps it will be another adventure. If we don't like it, we can always move back.

Frank, Shmulik, and I boarded an El Al plane in August 1979. I was eight months pregnant with our second child.

Now we are gathered in our living room—Frank, Shmulik, and our *sabarim* born in Israel: Yossi, Estie, Yehoshua and Miriam; Adi, Shachar, and Oriah. We are not saying much. The past two months have tied our tongues.

On Purim we celebrated the Persian king's annulment of his decree to kill all the Jews in his kingdom. But today there seems to be a new decree. Throughout Israel, every day, sometimes twice a day, Israelis have been murdered in their homes, in their yards, in their cars, while holding silver *kiddush* cups as they bless the wine. Babies have exploded in their strollers; their mothers have gone up in flames. Some Israelis have survived those attacks only to find they have lost their entire family— their spouse, all their children. Children have lost their parents, their brothers and sisters. The wounds of the living will take more than this lifetime to heal.

Sometimes the victims are not even Jewish but just happened to be in the restaurant or on the bus or on the crosswalk: Israeli Arabs, Chinese, Romanians. Even two TIPH observers (Temporary International Presence in Hebron), one from Turkey and one from Switzerland, were gunned down. The aim of the Muslim perpetrators is to bring the fiery Day of Judgment so that they may ascend to heaven as martyrs. Increasingly, the would-be martyrs are teenagers, sixteen-year-old Arab boys and girls who wear explosive belts under their shirts and with a tap turn life into purgatory.

In every attack there are victims whom we know or who knew our friends. Almost every attack occurs in a familiar place.

The Israeli people have not put on sackcloths and ashes as they did in Persia when King Ahashverus decreed the death of the Jews, but we mourn nonetheless. We cry out, "Enough of letting America tie our hands while she bombs the hell out of innocent civilians in Afghanistan. So what if America turns off her faucets of money? Wipe out the Palestinian Authority! To war! War!"

In the midst of crying for revenge and cleaning for Passover, Adi went into labor. Hours later in Jerusalem, she gave birth to a little girl whose name is Oriah, which means "Light of God."

Passover came in with brutal winds, white skies, and a downpour, foreboding things we do not know. Leaning on silk pillows like free men and women, no longer slaves, we drank sweet red wine in long-stemmed silver chalices. We proclaimed, "In our blood, we will live!"

Estie burst into the room, for she had opened the Internet and read: "At a hotel in Netanya, families who were just taking their places for the Passover Seder [before the matzot and red wine, the bitter herbs, and all the symbols of our exodus from Egypt] were blown to smithereens. A suicide bomber exploded himself."

Yet we went on with our Seder. Shmulik leads us in his alto voice through the Passover Haggadah. The Jews suffered in Egypt, which prepared them for a revelation of God. And in every generation thereafter our enemies have risen, and will rise, to wipe us out. But God will save us from them. We rose from the table at 1:30 in the morning, our strength and hopefulness renewed.

With that strength, we were able to face the stormy days ahead. Yossi became ill, and we took him to Hadassah Hospital. He had his head on Shmulik's lap in the emergency room when the bulletin appeared on television just after three o'clock in the afternoon, titled with forbidding red letters: Terrorist Attack. Suddenly before our eyes were the remains of what had been a busy restaurant in Haifa.

Within a half-hour the nurses and doctors in the emergency room knew from their colleagues working up north that this attack too had been cataclysmic. Before it was revealed to the public, we were told that at least fourteen people had been killed, if not more, and everyone in the restaurant had been injured when a bomber had blown himself up.

Watching televisions in the emergency room, I saw the unbearable pain of the past eighteen months reflected in the eyes of the people around me. But was it only from the past eighteen months? Didn't suffering follow the Jews around like a shadow? Pogroms, about which my mother had murmured in her delirium; persecutions through the ages; and the Holocaust—was that so long ago?

For years I had lamented this destiny. I had journeyed to find Indians, only to find *this* instead.

"I hope the doctors will come and examine Yossi before there is another terrorist attack," I said. Frank and Shmulik nodded. We all knew that in the event of an attack around Jerusalem, the injured would be brought to Hadassah Hospital,

182

and everyone waiting in the emergency room with their petty ailments would be pushed aside.

During the bulletin, a message flashed at the bottom of the screen: The border police were organizing a new unit to patrol the line between Arab and Israeli population centers. They were calling for volunteers. Anyone with military experience, regardless of age, could join. Frank took down the number for information.

Yossi had already received a draft notice as the IDF reserves were being mobilized for a major retaliatory military action against the terrorists nested inside the Palestinian Authority. He was in no shape to serve. Shmulik stood by his side when the doctor finally came to examine him. The doctors told us he had an acute case of Herpes virus.

"Keep him away from his wife and daughters until he's better. Take him home and nurse him back to health."

As we were leaving the hospital, another TV bulletin. In Efrat an Arab teenager had touched off his explosive belt in front of the first-aid center. Four people were seriously injured. They were being rushed to Hadassah Hospital in Jerusalem.

Medical personnel were already rolling the gurneys outside when we left. Nurses rushed about with bags of blood. The entrance to the trauma unit was cleared of visitors. As we walked outside, the sky was brown, full of sand. Drizzle splattered by our feet. Supporting Yossi, Shmulik led us to the car.

Estie's head is in my lap, and my head is on Shmulik's shoulder. Yossi looks in the refrigerator for something to eat. He lost ten pounds during his illness. Now that the sores in his mouth have healed, he wants to eat. Miriam makes him a salad. Yehoshua holds Shachar who is drinking her bottle. Orish is suckling at Adi's breast.

Estie was laid off again, from her second job, when Kentucky Fried Chicken closed its branch in Eilat. She had just moved into a new apartment. Now she will have to leave Eilat. Tourism is suffering; unemployment is on the rise.

The Israeli Defense Forces, in a massive operation called Defensive Wall, have driven into Arab cities and towns within the Palestinian Authority to wipe out the terrorists, to round up their weapons, to arrest those who surrender, to capture their leaders who plan the terror, to destroy factories where explosives are made. In Ramallah the IDF has taken over Yasir Arafat's headquarters; the chairman has been quarantined in the basement with his aides. Fierce battles are raging at Mukata and all around Ramallah, as well as in Jenin and Shechem. The IDF has also rolled into Bethlehem, Kalkilya, and Tulkarm.

Yossi's draft date has been moved up. At the end of April, Frank will go into the border police as a volunteer for two weeks. All around I see my neighbors in their green uniforms, kissing their children as they go off—twenty thousand IDF reserve soldiers have been drafted.

On my way to Jerusalem, near Bethlehem, I see young soldiers with all their gear climbing into armored personnel carriers. Palestinian gunmen are holding hostages inside the Church of the Nativity. The IDF has the church surrounded. Tanks with turrets aimed at Bethlehem fill the street. In this sector of Jerusalem there is no civilian traffic.

Two of my sons' friends were killed in the Operation—

Shmuel Weiss and Gedalia Mellick, both from Kiriat Arba. We visited their families to offer comfort.

"Was it worth it, Ema?" Estie wants to know. "Leaving America and coming here?"

I think for long minutes. All my experiences gather themselves into a point that sticks in my throat. "I guess. . . . I was brought here by forces beyond my control. I guess . . . this is where I'm supposed to be. Some people make decisions and their lives go according to plan. But my life wasn't like that."

"I have grown in ways I would never have realized anywhere else. I feel a spiritual dimension to my life that grows deeper every day." My fingers are in Estie's hair. "But the best part of having come to Israel is that, if we had stayed in America, we wouldn't have had you *sabarim*."

Frank pulls up a chair. "There is something I've been meaning to ask you kids. Look, you never asked to be born in Israel, or you, Shmulik, to immigrate here. Israel is such a difficult country to live in, and it seems it will get worse before it gets any better. Before Yehoshua gets drafted, I just want to give you a chance to decide finally if Israel is where we should live."

Miriam comes out of the kitchen with a knife in her hand. "Are you joking?"

"No. I read that Australia is encouraging immigration. We can get land there and connect to it like a Jew should, without all this mess."

Shmulik is the first to break the shocked silence. "I made my decision when I was in America last year. This is my country."

Yossi said, "There's no question, really. Ema, can you bring out the food?"

"Are you crazy?" Yehoshua asked. "I want to serve in the army in an elite unit. You want to deprive me of that?"

Estie sat up. "I was planning to live in America until Gandhi [Rehavam Ze'evi] was killed. Would he want his assassination to scare us out of Israel? No, this is where I will bring up my children."

"Me too." Miriam said.

"Adi, what about you?" Oriah stops suckling for a moment. "Leave Israel? Never in my life."

Frank admitted later that he knew this would be their answer. But he wanted them to confirm it.

Frank calls me outside, "Junie, quick, quick." It is just the two of us on this morning of the fifty-fourth Independence Day of Israel. Miriam is sleeping. Our other children have gone their own ways. Operation Defensive Wall has brought a lull in the terror.

"Listen," Frank puts a finger to his lips. The hills around Hebron are quiet. The doves are cooing. He points to the steep street that rises to the school. I see an Arab riding up the hill, atop a refrigerator that lies sideways on his wagon, drawn by his mule.

"*Alter Zachen! Alter Zachen!*" he cries out in Yiddish. "Old things. Old things to buy and sell." He is a relic of the days when Arabs and Jews lived together.

"I think those days will return, Junie. I think we'll be happy here yet."

Kiriat Arba, Hebron
April 26, 2002

A NOTE ON THE AUTHOR

June Leavitt was born in New York City and grew up on Long Island. She was graduated from the University of Wisconsin, Madison, in 1972, became a religious Jew in 1977, and two years later emigrated to Israel with her husband and two-year-old son. For the past twenty years, she has lived in Kiriat Arba, Hebron, raising her five children, writing and teaching English, though now she is a secular Jew. Her other books include *Flight to Seven Swan Bay*; *Vivre à Hebron,* a French edition of her 1991–1994 diary, also published in German; and *Cochav Nophel,* the Hebrew edition of her novel *Falling Star.*